The New Adults' Guide to Basic Finances

Written by Marjorie Daley

Illustrated by Madora Daley-Green

Daley Book

Dedication

For my kids Justin, Madora, and Will

Acknowledgment

A huge thank you to Kaia and Charlie Karleen. These young adults read the rough draft and made some invaluable comments that helped to make this book less confusing

Table of Contents

Introduction

Adulting can be really daunting. It is not just getting an apartment and doing your own laundry. There is money, taxes, insurance… the list keeps growing. Most of my experience comes from on-the-job learning.

Like many people, I was underprepared for handling my financial life – the two pieces of education my parents gave me were 1) do not spend too much money, and 2) always pay the vet and the feed store. Not very helpful! My initial goal for this was a simple one- or two- paragraph description that my own young adult children could use as a guide.

As I started writing and asked other long-term adults what they would have liked to have known or still struggle with, this book got longer and more complex.

This book should give you a sound start on understanding basic finances and hopefully help you not to make too many errors as you learn to manage your finances. Once you have the basics down, the rest will not seem as confusing or daunting.

Money management is like any other activity. If you put time into it, you will see a reward. If you avoid money management, you will not be good at it and you will not be financially successful.

You do not have to be a dragon, hoarding your money and polishing your scales, but if you spend just a bit of time managing your money, no one will be able to sneak in and steal your treasure.

1. Starting a Job

When you start a job, you will fill out two important forms. These are the W-4 which tells payroll how much money to withhold for federal taxes, and the I-9 which proves your legal ability to work in the US.

W-4

The W-4 is three pages long, but you only need to worry about page 1. The rest of the pages deal with claiming exemptions.

Exemptions are legal reductions that reduce the amount of taxable income. People often think exemptions are the same as deductions, but they are not. Unless you have a very specific reason to claim exemptions, always claim zero.

Exemptions allow you to pay less money to the Internal Revenue Service (IRS) because you have a lot of dependents or are the head of household (a legal definition). A dependent is dependent on you for shelter, food, etc. They are usually children, but not always.

The problem with claiming extra exemptions is that if your income or status changes, you may end up owing the IRS money. Declaring ZERO is a way to, in most cases, NOT have to pay the IRS at the end of the year.

If you think you should file exemptions, talk with a tax preparer like a Certified Public Accountant (CPA) to get the specific pros and cons. There have been many changes recently and there will always be changes created by our federal legislators.

I-9

In order to work legally in the US, you must be a citizen, a naturalized citizen, a lawful permanent citizen, or have a worker's visa. You must present the proper identification to fill out the I-9. You will need:

- U.S. Passport or U.S. Passport Card

OR

- One of the following: driver's license or government-issued ID card or school ID with photograph (there are others, but these are the most common)

AND

- One of the following: Social Security account card; certified record of birth or birth certificate; Form I-179 card; or Employment authorization issued by the Department of Homeland Security

2. Checking Accounts

If you have never had a checking account, it is time to open one. Find a bank or a credit union and apply to open a checking account - you may not need the checks, but they all come with debit cards.

A checking account is a place to keep your money and access it without having to carry cash. Most checking accounts do not come with interest, so it is not a great place to store a lot of money long-term. When you open a checking account you will be offered checks and/or a debit card. These are how you will access your money.

You will also be able to use an ATM to get cash. The ATM takes money directly out of your checking account. You are assessed a variety of fees for using ATMs.

When you use a check or debit card, your bank takes money out of your account and transfers it to the other person's bank and account. If you do not have enough money in your account to cover the check or debit, your bank will charge you fees to cover the difference or will "bounce" the check back to the check receiver. The vendor will be fined for your bounced check, and they pass it on to you as a returned check or insufficient fund penalty. Bouncing checks can end up costing you a lot. Plus, using a check when you know there is not enough money to cover the check can result in criminal charges. If you are using a debit card, the debit card transaction will fail to complete.

I strongly urge you to learn to balance your checkbook. That will save you in fees and penalties. There are several apps, like Mint, that can help you to balance your checkbook.

You may not need many checks because most people and places take debit cards or use a pay platform. Debit cards are sort of like credit cards except that your debit card immediately takes money out of your checking account. I will discuss the safety aspects of credit cards and debit cards in the Scams and Data Breaches section.

Voided Check

If your employer offers direct deposit, you will supply them with a voided check. Write VOID in big letters across the face of the check. This gives the payroll department all the information they need to put money into your account. This includes your bank account number, the proper name of the account (how your name appears), and the bank's routing number (the bank's electronic "address").

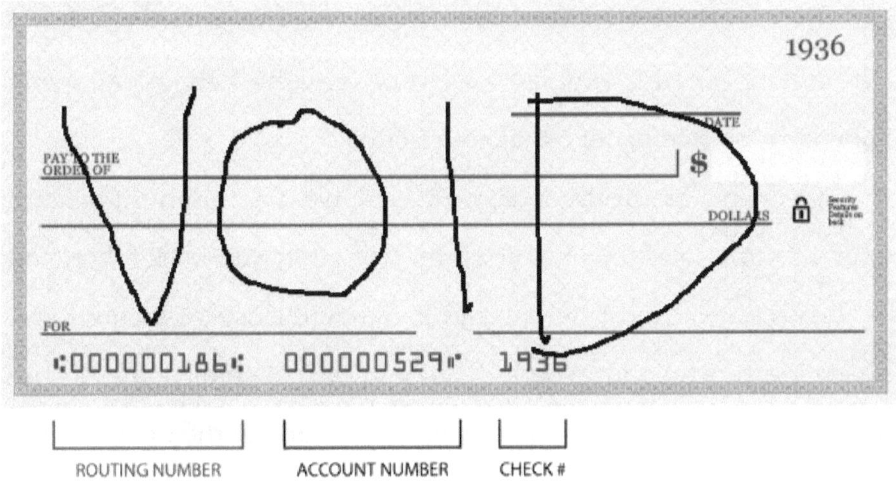

Banks Versus Credit Unions

After banking for a lot of decades, I have very strong opinions about banks and credit unions. I will never bank at a traditional bank for several reasons, but you need to make the best choice for your situation. Here's the low down.

Ownership

Banks are money-making operations owned by shareholders. Credit unions are not-for-profit organizations that are owned by members (account holders). The bank needs to show a profit to their shareowners while credit unions do not need to earn profits for the owners. This distinction makes a difference in the interest rates and use of fees by the institution.

You usually must be a member of a specific group to join a credit union, such as a county employee to join the county employee credit union. Credit unions are very creative about allowing membership, so that is not usually an issue.

To open a credit union account, you need a minimum balance in your account - about $5 per account. You get the $5 back when you close the account. Credit unions and banks will close an account that has been inactive for a long period, but you can ask to have the closure reversed and get back the money. It does not work all the time, but it is worth asking.

Fees

Banks have a lot of fees. Banks and credit unions will charge one or more of the fees listed below, although credit unions tend to have fewer fees overall. If you are not aware of the fees, you can end up losing a lot of money.

Both types of institutions charge fees such as overdraft and insufficient funds. Banks often charge more of the fees listed below. Fees include but are not limited to:

Service fees - charged to keep your account open (you are already letting them use your money)

Maintenance fees - these include inactivity fees and minimum balance fees. If your account is inactive, they can take a certain amount each month to "keep the account open." It is possible to drain an account with inactive fees. Minimum balance fees mean you must keep a certain amount of money in your account. If you fall below that amount, they charge you a fee for not having enough money in your account.

Overdraft fees - these are charged when you do not have enough money in your account to cover a purchase. The bank will cover your purchase and then charge you an overdraft fee, often $35 per overdraft. If you make two charges on your account, and both are overdrafts, you will be charged $70.

Insufficient fund fee - this is charged if you do not have enough money in your account and do not have overdraft protection.

ATM fees - using the ATM linked to a different bank to get your money out. There can be two fees for this, one from the bank's ATM and from your bank. It can get very expensive!

Wire transfer fee - if you send money from one bank to another, one or both banks may charge a fee for the transfer.

International transaction fees - these kick in if you use a debit card in another country.

Products

Traditionally, banks offer more "products" like mortgages, loans, business credit cards, etc. than do credit unions. This is rapidly changing, so whatever product you want, you will probably find it at a credit union.

Interest Rates

There are two different interest rates. One is charged to you when you use someone else's money. The other is given to you when the bank uses your money to lend to other people.

Financial institutions make money by lending money to other financial institutions and to other people. If you take out a car loan, your loan is not coming from the bank's money. It is coming from other people who have checking accounts at the bank. The interest you pay is then paid back to the people who lent you the money.

If you would like a great example of how banks lending money to other people benefits everyone, watch *It's a Wonderful Life*.

Because banks work for their shareholders, not their account holders, you will have lower interest rates paid to you (savings accounts) and higher interest rates charged if you take out a loan from the bank. Credit unions offer slightly higher interest rates on savings accounts and lower interest rates on their car loans and mortgages because they are working for their account holders.

Online Services

Banks are generally considered to have better online services than do credit unions. In my experience, it depends on the credit union!

Safety

Both banks and credit unions are insured by the FDIC (Federal Deposit Insurance Corp) to $250,000 per account. This means you will not lose your money to a bank failure or robbery.

Customer Service

Here is where I choose credit unions over banks. I have found that most credit unions have a far superior level of customer service. Even when I lived in a huge city, the credit union tellers made an effort to remember my name. I have never had that level of service from a bank. When I have had issues at my credit union, I had meetings with the president of the credit union. Try that as a small account holder at a bank!

Locations

In general, major banks have more locations and ATMs in the same city and sometimes nationwide. That can be a huge plus if you travel a lot.

In addition to brick-and-mortar financial institutions, there are many online only banks. The online banks are often a very good option because they offer higher interest on your savings and checking accounts since they do not have to pay for buildings and staff. You may not get many products and there is no customer service to speak of.

I use an online bank to store my emergency funds. It takes two to three days to have the money transferred to my checking account. This helps keep me from making impulse purchases with my emergency funds. My active-duty son has an online account for his eventual car purchase.

Regardless of which you choose, ALWAYS know what you are signing up for.

3. Understanding Your Pay Stub

Pay stubs are a record of what you made and the taxes you have had taken out. Employers make errors, so check your pay stub for accuracy.

The following pay stub is a sample of how yours might look.

A Daley Book
Laramie WY

EARNING STATEMENT

EMPLOYEE NAME / ADDRESS				SSN	REPORTING PERIOD	PAY DATE	#
Financial Dragon				xxx-xx-1234	12/13/2020 - 12/19/2020	12/20/2020	Employee # 4321
INCOME	RATE	HOURS	CURRENT PAY	DEDUCTIONS		TOTAL	YTD TOTAL
GROSS EARNING	$10	40	$400.00	STATUTORY DEDUCTIONS			
				FICA - MEDICARE		$5.80	$295.80
				FICA- SOCIAL SECURITY		$24.80	$1,264.80
				FEDERAL TAX		$44.50	$2,269.50
				STATE TAX		$0.00	$0.00
YTD GROSS	YTD DEDUCTIONS	YTD NET PAY		TOTAL		DEDUCTIONS	NET PAY
$20,400.00	$3,830.10	$16,569.90		$400.00		$75.10	$324.90

Regardless of if you get a mailed or emailed pay stub, they all contain the same basic information.

Your Pay Stub

Your pay stub should have the following information.

Personal information including:

- Employer name and address
- Employee - make sure it is you! If there is a social security number, make certain it is yours
- Your department or title
- Date the check was issued or direct deposited

Payment information including:

- Base Rate of Pay
- Current Pay Summary or Earnings and Hours
- Pay period
- Deductions and net pay
- Earnings Details- if you have variable pay or received tips,

your breakdown is here. It will include your regular hours, overtime hours, vacation, sick time or PTO used, and tips

Tax information including:

- Insurance – if offered
- FICA (Federal Insurance Contributions Tax) - may be labeled as social security, SS, or retirement
- FICA - may be labeled as Medicare or MC - withheld for federal health insurance
- Federal Withholding (FIT) - these are your federal income taxes
- Any withholdings for retirement accounts
- Any state, county, and city withholdings

Year to Date (YTD) summary including:

- Earnings
- Taxes
- Deductions
- Net pay

Benefits summary which will depend on your employer's benefits package. You may have none. Benefits include:

- Paid Time Off (PTO) sometimes offered instead of vacation and sick time
- Vacation
- Sick Time
- Extended Illness benefit

Gross and Net Pay

The concept of gross pay and net pay is very important. Gross pay is what you make before taxes. Net pay or take-home pay is what you get after taxes are taken out. To keep them straight, gross means big or large. Net is what you take home after you pull a fishing net out of the water and all the excess water drains away and little fishes fall out.

4. Budgeting

Now that you have a checking account and income, the next step is to figure out how to spend your money. The single most important financial action you should take is to create and live by a budget. A budget tracks your income and expenditures and allows you to control where your money is going and to plan for the future.

Whether or not you have a strict budget that you keep to by the penny or just a general idea of where your money is going is up to your personality and needs. The important part is knowing where and how much you are spending.

Money is like any other activity – the more time you put into it, the larger the return. Budgeting can be difficult and managing money means you might not be able to splurge on a want. If you invest time into managing your money, you will see a return in increased savings and decreased debt.

Wants Versus Needs

Before setting up a budget, you need to identify the difference between wants and needs. This will guide your budget. A need is something that is necessary to your survival. This includes food, shelter, clothing, and your health. A want is not essential to survival but makes surviving much more pleasant.

If you are not sure if something is a need or a want, here is a list of questions to ask yourself BEFORE you make a purchase, especially one that is large. How much "large" is depends on your unique situation. It could be as little as $5 or as much as many thousands.

1) Is This a Need or a Want?

Very often, wants and needs have some sort of overlap, and these are areas that you can adjust to help you meet your budget. For instance, an apartment is a need - it is shelter. Choosing an apartment because of the desirability of an address or for amenities that you may not use but are really cool are wants. A car for transportation is a need, but the newest model or most expensive trim is a want.

If you can afford a want without hurting yourself financially, still take the time to consider the following questions. Mindless spending can have a huge impact on your financial future.

2) Can I Wait 24 Hours?

Hard selling is a skill that successful salespeople learn. They know that if you walk out on a potential purchase that you probably will not be back to buy it. That is also why marketers create such a hype around new versions of the same old thing. If your purchase is not an emergency and you can wait 24 hours, you 1) do not need it, and 2) are making an impulse purchase.

If it is a deal too good to pass up, go back to question #1.

3) Can I Afford It?

If your answer is "no," walk away. If your answer is "maybe," can you pay cash or pay off a credit card before the grace period is over? If not, walk away.

A sub-question in this category is whether the purchase will hurt your ability to afford a need in the future. For example, if your car tires are nearing the end of their life expectancy and you know you must replace them, can you afford that gaming system right now? If buying that want will keep you from affording a need, you cannot afford it.

4) *How Long Did It Take to Earn the Money?*

Your time has value, so try looking at the purchase in light of how many hours it took you to earn the money. Let's say you have your eye on the newest gaming system. It is priced at $500. If you make the federal minimum wage of (as of now) $7.25 per hour, that gaming system costs you 68 hours of your work-life. If you are working 40 hours a week, that represents almost 2 weeks of your life. Is that gaming system worth two weeks of your life?

5) *What are the Additional Costs?*

The least expensive part of buying a car (and especially a house) or a pet is the purchase price. You will lay out a lot more over the life of the car, house, or pet than you paid for it. Suppose you are looking for a car and your choice is between a used BMW and a Ford. You will spend far more for that high-end BMW than you will for the Ford. The BMW technicians are more expensive, the routine maintenance is more expensive, the parts - even the windshield - are more expensive. And your car insurance will be more expensive.

A hidden additional cost is the fees and interest rate accrual that occur when you use a credit card to make purchases. These hidden costs can add up very quickly.

If you use a credit card to purchase your $500 gaming system and you do not pay it off immediately, you end up paying more for your gaming system. I will go over the ins and outs of credit cards in greater detail, but here is a fast example.

Cost of gaming system: $500

Interest rate: 21.21%

Minimum payment $25

Time to pay off: 25 months

Interest paid: $122.42

Actual cost: $622.40

Your 68 hours of work-life plus credit card charges have become more than two full weeks of income.

The sub-question in this category is "what else can I spend this money on?" If you spend $50 a week on groceries, that $622 represents 12 weeks of groceries.

You might be better off saving up that $500 toward new car tires or so you can pay cash for your gaming system. If the costs are more than you can afford, this item is a want.

6) Is This the Best Value?

Yes, it is exciting to buy new, but this is not a good reason to buy new when used works just as well. The instant you drive a brand-new car off the lot you cannot sell the car for what you just paid for it. This is known as depreciation or loss of value. If you buy a gently used car, someone else has taken the depreciation for you.

If you love designer clothing, many larger cities have high-end used clothing boutiques that offer amazing deals on gently used designer clothing.

Research different stores including online venues. If you are looking at a big-ticket item, check out both positive and negative reviews as well as publications like *Consumer Reports*. You might be buying a name-brand item that has a reputation as a "lemon." But beware of the overly cheap item such as your brand-new gaming system offered for $150 – it is probably a scam.

7) Where am I Going to Put This?

If you are buying something large or alive, ask where you are going to put it and if you have time for it. If you are eyeing an animal, is it the right animal for your situation? Are you willing to put the time into the animal? Will that piece of furniture actually fit through the door?

8) Is There a Return Policy?

Ask about the return policy. Some companies charge a restocking fee or offer store credit instead of refunds so you may want to skip the purchase until you are certain you want it. Check on warranties and recalls because of defective manufacturing.

If you are not 100% certain you want the item, but you buy it anyway, the odds are you will eventually regret the purchase.

9) Does This Have a Use?

This question is particularly useful when deciding whether to buy a knickknack (or gifting one). Think of all the dust catchers that take up space. You could probably lose them all and never miss them. Not everything has to be useful but buying items because they are there is not cost-effective. One or two items are generally nicer than a dozen. And think about packing up all that stuff when you move.

10) Have I Regretted Purchases in the Past?

If you have a closet, garage, or a room in your parent's house full of regrets, you may have an issue with impulse shopping. Slow down, take your time, work through the questions above and make an informed decision.

Now that you can identify wants versus needs, it is time to move on to budgeting.

Types of Budgets

There are dozens of budget styles and concepts available that will fit your personality and attention to detail. No matter which budget you use, they all start with the same general steps.

A budget will identify how much income you have as well as your needs and wants and will help you set up a savings plan. Once you identify all your expenses, compare those to your income and, for most people, start decreasing expenditures where you are overspending.

I particularly like the 50/30/20 budget for its simplicity. The basis of this budget is that you spend 50% of your income on needs, 30% on wants, and 20% goes into savings.

Make a budget and see if it fits into the 50/30/20 budget. If you brought your needs in under 50%, congratulations. If you did not, you will need to cut some expenses. If you did not hit your 30% wants goal, it is time to cut costs. Drop cable, look for a cheaper phone and/or phone plan, find a cheaper internet company, learn how to do your own manicures, etc. Where you cut depends on you.

The savings percentage is further divided into savings, emergencies, retirement, future purchases, and debt payoff. You can have more than one savings account! I will detail each type under savings.

Depending on your personality and focus on detail, you can find a budget to fit your needs. The biggest factor for success is that you

write it down and pay attention to where you are spending your money.

The Worksheet section contains budgeting worksheets, so once you have grasped the concepts in this book, you can turn to the worksheet and start on your own.

Budgeting Worksheets and Apps

There are free and paid apps available. Two free ones include Mint or Clarity Money. Both had good reviews and seemed simple. If you prefer the computer method, look at Mint Lifestyle, GoogleSheets or Excel templates. My middle child uses a simple Excel spreadsheet to track their expenses and income very effectively and cheaply.

Next Steps

In the next five sections, I will discuss specific sections that you will need to address in your budget, including savings accounts, insurance, investing, retirement, and taxes.

5. Savings and Savings Accounts

As you budget for your 30% or if you find extra money, plan for what you intend to do with the money. Savings accounts have very low interest rates, so you can find online accounts or investments with better interest rates as you save up more money.

Most banks and credit unions will let you open more than one savings account and label them with your own goal. Consider having six different savings accounts, each with a different goal. Your first one will be a general savings account.

General Savings Account

A general savings account is a holding place for money you are planning to move to another account in the future. You should maintain a minimum amount in it (initial goal is $100 with a final goal of $1,000) and tie it to your checking account so if you accidentally bounce a check, you will not get hit with an insufficient fund fee.

Emergency Fund

This fund is only for emergencies! This means car breakdowns, job loss, medical emergencies, etc. Your initial goal is $1000 with a final goal of three months of income. As you increase your earnings, you will want to adjust your emergency savings accordingly. If you prefer concrete numbers, Bankrate suggests goals for emergency savings goals by age as follows:

Age	Emergency saving goal
30	$10,368 to $20,736
40	$12,900 to $25,800
50	$13,158 to $26,316
60	$11,598 to $23,196

Having an emergency fund is a key financial strategy to avoid accumulating debt.

Retirement Fund

Even if you have a retirement fund through work, you can always set up another retirement fund. This can get pretty confusing so I will discuss the different types of retirement accounts in more detail. However, start your retirement savings account with an initial goal of $1000. When you reach that goal, transfer it to your formal retirement account and then start building it up again.

Future Purchases

What are you saving for? A new car? Vacation? Laptop? Here is where that money goes. The goal is your own and the speed you build it depends on your income and expenditures.

Annual Set Aside

The annual set aside is for annual expenses like car and health insurance (if not paid monthly), car licenses and tags. Before I started an annual set aside savings account, I was regularly caught short on insurance payments and license fees. Now, I set aside 1/12 of the annual expenses every month. It is a rolling balance, so there is no goal and the relief for me from doing this has been tremendous! I check the annual total needed once a year and adjust the monthly deposits as needed.

Debt Payoff

If you have debt, make the minimum payments through your needs budget, but then save up money to pay down debt. There are several different methods to pay down debt, which will be discussed in greater detail.

Freezing Savings Accounts

Most credit unions will allow you to put a freeze on your savings accounts. For instance, you can set a $1000 freeze on your emergency account which means you can withdraw the balance to that $1000 freeze point, but no more. The freeze can be easily lifted with a phone call to the credit union. If you spend money like water, a freeze is a good way to stop yourself from rashly spending money.

6. Insurance

Insurance is one of those adulting things that is pretty baffling, very important, and subject to a lot of misunderstanding. Basically, you purchase insurance to protect you when bad things happen, and the insurance companies sell you insurance hoping that nothing bad will happen. They have your risks calculated to many decimals and employ a lot of statisticians called actuaries who make certain that you pay more than they pay out.

Types of Insurance

Life Insurance

Life insurance offers your beneficiaries a certain amount that is paid when you die. Beneficiaries are people who "benefit" from your death. The concept behind life insurance is to replace the income that would be lost if you died.

When you enroll in a life insurance program, you will probably have a medical examination, and your premiums (what you pay each month or year for the policy) are based on your health, age, sex, and job description. Some may take into account hobbies, especially if you skydive, scuba dive, or participate in other risky sports. The younger you are when you enroll, the less expensive the premiums. In addition, you do not own your policy, your beneficiary does.

There are two types - whole life and term life. Whole life is paid to your beneficiaries when you die. You pay a certain number of premiums and after that, the whole life policy stays in effect for the amount that you purchased. This is called the face value.

Whole life comes with a built-in "savings account." Out of every premium you pay, part of it goes toward the policy and part into the savings account. If you get into financial trouble, you can borrow from this savings account. While that sounds like a great idea, the insurance company will charge you interest on the amount you borrow. In addition, your heirs will only get the face value of your policy on your death and not the amount held in the savings account.

Term life insurance is for a certain amount of time and then expires. Term life is far less expensive than whole life because it is only for a limited duration. For instance, you may want to get term life insurance that covers you until your children turn 18.

There are two other types of life insurance: child life and final expenses.

Taking out a life insurance policy on a child is generally regarded as a waste of money. First, the death rate for children is statistically very low. Second, you are not dependent on that child for income. The main reason to purchase child life insurance is if you have a family history of chronic illnesses like diabetes. Child life insurance can be rolled into an adult plan while purchasing life insurance with a chronic disease as an adult is much more expensive.

Final expense insurance is designed to help your loved ones take care of your remains. Cemetery plots and especially coffins are very expensive, so if you want a fancy funeral, final expense insurance can help offset the cost.

Do you need life insurance? If you have dependents or are planning to start a family in the near future, yes, consider a term life policy. Otherwise, hold off on this expense.

Health Insurance

Health insurance is a huge controversial topic. I will explain the basics as they stand at the end of 2020, with the warning that all this may change. There are a number of different health insurance options: employer, private, Affordable Care Act (ACA)/Obamacare, Medicare, and Medicaid.

Employer insurance is offered through your employer, and you may pay for all or part of the cost.

Private insurance is purchased through an insurance company and covers just you (and your dependents).

ACA/Obamacare is defined by the federal government and offered by private insurance companies as an option for people who do not fall into the first two categories.

Medicare is federal health insurance for people over 65. Medicaid is federal health insurance for people who fall below the federal poverty level.

With the exception of Medicare and Medicaid, the other three types are very similar. The basics are as follows: you will have a deductible, a copay, possibly a cap, and possibly pre-existing conditions.

The deductible is a set amount that you will have to pay out of pocket each year. If you have a $1000 deductible, you will pay for the first $1000 of medical care every year. At that point, insurance will pay, usually, between 80% and 100% of your medical bills for the rest of the year.

Your deductible will determine your premium. The lower the deductible, the more expensive the insurance. If you have a high deductible, you have catastrophic insurance because it will only cover you if you suffer a medical catastrophe like a serious car accident or other serious injury/illness.

The co-pay is an out-of-pocket expense that you pay at every doctor visit. Usually, the co-pay is applied toward the 20% not covered by your insurance company.

A cap is a lifetime limit on insurance. Your insurance company may cap your coverage at $1 million. Once you hit that $1 million, you will not be able to get health insurance. While this may seem like a lot of money, in the current health industry it is not. Cancer, severe accidents, and chronic illnesses rapidly eat up the cap. If you have a child with a chronic illness or cancer, they may meet their cap in a few years and never be insurable again.

Pre-existing conditions are those that predate your insurance coverage. This can include, quite literally, anything that has ever happened to you but are commonly cancers and chronic health issues. A COVID-19 infection may be considered a pre-existing condition in the future, although that is not certain at this time.

As an example of the unreasonableness of pre-existing conditions, I had an arthroscope and kneecap release (very common surgeries) under an employer-provided insurance policy. When I applied for private health insurance, my knee was considered a pre-existing condition by the insurance company and the company refused to cover anything that involved my knee. I could have medical treatment above or below the joint, but not the joint itself, regardless of if the injury was related to the surgery.

ACA/Obamacare eliminated the pre-existing condition and cap situation for everyone. Unfortunately, this may change in the near future as the ACA is constantly being dismantled by our federal lawmakers.

It is very important to keep up your health insurance coverage so as not to be refused for pre-existing conditions. If you have coverage through work and quit, two things will happen. One, you will get a letter that states the dates of your coverage. Do not lose this letter! It proves you are insurable to the next insurance company.

Secondly, you will be offered COBRA insurance. This is the option to purchase health insurance through your former employer until you find other insurance. The joke is that it is called COBRA because it will bite you. COBRA insurance is fantastically expensive and should only be used as a last resort.

Currently, you can look for health insurance online. The insurance company needs to be registered in your state so always check that. You may have a network of health care providers that you must use, so make certain there are providers in your area.

If you want to enroll in ACA/Obamacare, at this point, there is a website to use to sign up. However, there is a window (dates where you can enroll). Currently, this is a six-week window that begins in November and ends in December.

If you qualify for Medicaid, you will apply through your state's Medicaid department.

Another important issue about insurance is that eye and dental care is not included and must be purchased separately.

Do you need health insurance? Yes, no matter your age or health status.

Car/Vehicle Insurance

If you thought that health insurance was confusing, just wait until I get into car insurance! There are four types of US states: tort, no-fault, verbal threshold, and no insurance required. Since the no insurance required list is very short, let's eliminate them right off. At the time of writing, Virginia and New Hampshire do not require car/vehicle insurance unless you are driving a financed car (one you have leased or have a loan on).

No-fault states require you to buy car insurance that covers damages to YOUR car and you and your passengers. These states are Kansas, Kentucky, Hawaii, Massachusetts, Minnesota, Utah, North Dakota, Florida, Michigan, New Jersey, New York, and Pennsylvania. The benefits of living in a no-fault state are that the claims payouts (getting money from your insurance company) are faster, there are fewer lawsuits, and lower insurance premiums. In the first seven states, you cannot easily sue another driver for compensation.

Of those no-fault states, Florida, Michigan, New Jersey, New York, and Pennsylvania are verbal threshold states. These states require a whole or partial loss of a body member (eye, leg, etc.) or whole or partial loss of function to occur before there can be a lawsuit. You need to buy personal injury protection insurance to make up any short falls in compensation to the other driver.

All other states fall into the tort category. In this category, you are buying insurance to pay the other driver if you cause the accident. If you are at fault, you can be sued for medical bills, pain, suffering, and damages.

Every tort or verbal threshold state has a different requirement for insurance minimums; however, most states require a minimum of liability insurance. Liability protects the other drivers in case you cause a wreck that damages their car, or they are injured.

The next three coverages are optional unless the car is financed. You will be required to have liability and collision until your car is paid in full. Collision repairs your car if you cause an accident. Comprehensive covers your car from weather, theft, and other damages. Medical coverage supplements your health insurance and that of your passengers in the case you or they are injured in a wreck. Under-insured driver kicks in if the other driver does not have enough insurance to cover the damage to you or your car.

Choosing limits and deductibles will determine how much your insurance costs and how effective it is.

Let's say you back into a telephone pole and your car is dented. If you have liability only, you can make no claim against your insurance. If you have collision coverage, you can make a claim and the insurance company may pay to have the car repaired.

You take the car to the body shop and get an estimate for $1500. You submit the claim to your insurance, and they will either pay it or deny it. The insurance company decides to pay. Like all insurances, there is a deductible. In this case, it is $500. You pay the $500 and the insurance pays $1000. Your deductible is set when you buy the insurance and the lower the deductible, the more expensive the insurance.

Because cars and other vehicles lose value, insure your car for collision, comprehensive, and under-insured for the amount they are worth. If you have a $1,000 car insured for $5,000, you are losing money. The insurance company is not going to lay out $5,000 to repair or replace your $1,000 car. Comprehensive is probably not worth the cost on older, lower-value vehicles.

Medical coverage can be very important. As I discussed under health insurance, it does not take much of a serious injury to run up some really expensive medical bills. If you are in an accident, whether you are at fault or not, and your passengers are injured, you can be sued and end up having to pay a lot of Another factor to figure in is your age. Statistically, young male drivers cause more accidents than any other age and gender. If you are young and male, you will pay for car insurance! Once you hit age 25, your insurance rates drop.

If you have a lot of claims or traffic tickets, your insurance rates will go up because you are obviously a statistical risk for the insurance company.

Do you need car/vehicle insurance? Yes.

Mortgage Insurance and Homeowner's Insurance
Mortgage and homeowner's insurance are something you only have to worry about when you buy a house!

Renter's Insurance
If you rent, you should consider a renter's policy. Your landlord will have a policy that covers the building, but your stuff is not included. A renter's policy protects your belongings from loss, theft, water damage, vandalism, fire, smoke, and lightning. Occasionally, your landlord will provide or require renter's insurance. Always carefully read the lease before you sign it.

Renter's insurance covers personal possessions, liability (a guest gets hurt in your apartment), and additional living expenses. There are two riders (additional insurance) you can purchase: medical payments to others and extended coverage.

Personal Property Coverage is for items like clothing, furniture, and electronics. Your personal property coverage limits should be at or near the total value of your belongings. Generally, items are covered no matter where they are. If you are at class when your laptop is taken, you should be covered. Make certain you understand your policy.

Liability Coverage protects you if someone is injured by your actions in your apartment. Standard renter's insurance policy legal liability coverage covers tenants up to $100,000, although higher coverage is available.

Additional Living Expenses/Loss of Use covers your living expenses if your rental is damaged, and you are temporarily displaced.

Medical Payments to Others covers medical costs for a guest who is injured in your rental.

Extended Coverage is available if you have something particularly valuable. This includes expensive items like high-end jewelry, fur coats, etc.

Do you need renter's insurance? Maybe. Do you have a lot to replace? Do you have a lot of visitors? Could someone put you up temporarily if your apartment has a fire?

Accidental Death and Dismemberment Insurance

Accidental death and dismemberment insurance pay out for certain covered deaths, but not all. Overall, only 5.4% of deaths in the US in 2016 were the result of accidents. This means the insurance company is going to make money because the odds are that you are not going to die from an accident in any given year.

The dismemberment part covers loss of all or part of a limb, hearing or eyesight, or becoming paralyzed. While these can be extremely expensive injuries, they are also very rare.

If you are offered this benefit free as part of your employment, take it. Otherwise, this is probably not an important expense.

Disability Insurance

Disability insurance covers you if you are sick or injured and miss work for an extended period of time. Disabilities can include both physical and mental disabilities like mental illnesses. Always read your policy to understand what is covered. The insurance will cover 50-60% of your income. There are two types of disability insurance: short-term and long-term.

Short-term disability will pay for up to a year if you have a qualifying illness or injury. Long-term disability can replace part of your income for months or years, depending on your policy. The cost is generally 1 to 3% of your annual income for both.

If you feel better with a disability policy, purchase long-term disability. Otherwise, take 1% to 3% of your income and invest it against a short-term disability.

Pet Insurance

Pet insurance can be useful. In terms of emergency care, unless you have an animal that is earning a lot of money at shows or as a stud/ dam, or is a trained service dog, you need to decide on a reasonable amount of money you will spend on your pet for one emergency. When the emergency occurs, ask yourself 1) how old is the animal; 2) what is the probable outcome for the animal; and 3) how much pain will the animal be in?

It is probably better to have an emergency vet account than it is to take out pet insurance.

Travel Insurance

If you are planning an expensive trip, consider travel insurance. Travel insurance can cover trip cancellation, theft, medical treatment, relocation, and a 24-hour helpline for translation services.

Trip cancellation can help you recover non-refundable tickets or accommodations if you cancel the trip. Be sure to read your policy as not every reason for canceling is covered. Covid-19 outbreaks are presently not covered, but other illnesses are. Again, read and understand what is covered and how to go about proving the reason for the cancellation.

Theft coverage can help you recover the value of items stolen overseas or if your luggage is lost.

If your health insurance does not cover international health care, you can purchase medical treatment insurance. Before you leave the US, contact your health insurance company to see if you are covered.

If you are traveling and something like a civil war or a tsunami occurs in the country you are visiting, travel insurance can help you get out. Do not depend on the American Embassy to help. You are not their priority. And finally, some travel policies have 24-hour helplines to help with translating issues if you end up needing to see a doctor or even just get lost.

If you make reservations using your credit card, you may already have travel insurance as some credit cards offer this as a perk.

Do you need travel insurance? Yes, especially if you are planning an expensive trip. Check your credit card because it may have travel insurance as a perk when you make reservations through your credit card.

A Final Word on Insurance Companies

Do not be fooled by how "friendly" insurance companies and their salespeople may seem to be. They are not on your side. They are on the side of their stockholders and some companies will do what they can to not pay you. Understand what you are buying, what is covered, and how to make a claim. Do not be afraid to ask questions because insurance is complicated.

7. Investing

Investing is important. It is a way to make your money make money. This section will help you understand the terms and to speak with an adviser (or more importantly to pick one out). I will not go in-depth on how to invest because I am not an expert.

Basic savings accounts are not good places to keep money because you will not make a lot of interest. Instead, you want to look at other places to keep your money that have the potential to build wealth. In addition, if you have a retirement account, you will need to choose how to invest your money.

Bank Investing

Banks and credit unions offer savings accounts, CDs (certificates of deposit) and money market accounts. A **savings account** offers you a very low interest rate, usually figured quarterly (every three months), for the bank to use your money.

A **CD** is an account where you set aside a certain amount of money for a certain amount of time. CDs are advertised using APY instead of APR. The APY (annual percentage yield) includes the APR and the compounding effect.

For instance, you may need to put away $1,000 for five years. Your APY is 1.40% and it is compounded monthly. At the end of 5 years, your $1000 is now worth $1071.99. Frankly, that is not a lot of money, and you cannot use that $1000 for five years. You get slightly more interest than with a savings account, but you cannot touch your money until the CD matures and the interest is added.

A **money market** is, for you, a savings account with better interest rates. For the banks, it is a series of short-term loans between banks. Your money is the basis for the loan. A money market interest rate is slightly higher than a traditional savings account. Checking is available with some money market accounts, but there are usually some restrictions on how many checks you can write and for how much.

Those are the vehicles that banks offer. If you start to accrue more than a couple thousand dollars, it is time to move it into vehicles that make more money, in other words, investing. There is more risk involved (meaning there is a chance you may lose your money), but you can choose the level of risk you are comfortable with. Let's discuss investing.

Stocks, Bonds, and Mutual Funds

A **stock** represents ownership in a company. If you own a stock, you own a small part of the business, and the business pays you a dividend periodically. A dividend is a percentage of the profits.

Financial Dragon owns the company Hoarders. He needs to raise capital (money) to expand the business. He decides to offer 2,000 shares. Since he does not want to lose control of his company, he keeps 1,001 shares and sells 999 for $100 apiece. He now has $99,900. At the end of the year, he has a profit of $100,000 so he offers a dividend. His investors, the stockholders, each get a percentage of the profit per stock. If your dividend is 5%, each share would earn $2.50. If you own 100 shares, you earn $250.00.

Stocks range from extremely safe (blue-chip stocks) to incredibly risky (penny stocks). What you invest in depends on your comfort level and how much money you feel you can afford to lose.

Bonds are loans offered by governments and corporations to raise money to fund a project. When you purchase a bond, you are lending the government or corporation your money for a set amount of time. It is paid back in one lump sum, plus interest, when the bond matures. One example would be War Bonds sold by the United States government to help fund war efforts during WWI and WWII.

In a more contemporary example, you are a city manager and need to upgrade the sewer system. One way to raise the money to do this is to offer a bond. People buy the bonds and then you, the government, uses the money to build the project. When the bond matures, the investors get back their money plus interest. Bonds are generally considered safe but not particularly good investments because of very low interest rates. Governments generally do not default on bonds, but they can and have done so by declaring bankruptcy.

Mutual funds are groups of stocks and bonds put together by a portfolio manager. In this instance, a portfolio is a group of stocks and bonds. You buy into the mutual fund and get a percentage of the dividends. There are a variety of mutual funds including index funds which must be invested according to preset rules. Some mutual funds are blue-chip (very safe companies), some are topical such as wind energy, pharmaceutical companies, or other groups. Some involve a lot of risk. In general, mutual funds are pretty safe because you own a bit of a lot of companies and if one fails, you only lose a small part of your investment.

Hedge funds are an investment partnership. The partnership pools together money and someone then invests it. These are very risky and very expensive. Hedge funds are not for the beginner investor!

Buying into the Market

Once you have decided to invest, you can buy stocks on your own, you can buy from a stockbroker, or you can go with a Registered Investment Adviser. Personally, any time I have researched, selected, and bought stock; the company has immediately lost all value. It is not worth my time to master all the intricacies of stock trading, so I have an investment adviser. If stock trading is your interest, do a lot of studying!

Stockbrokers buy and sell investments. They make a commission either per trade or as a percentage of your assets held by their company. This is known as a load. If they make a fee per transaction, you run the risk that they will recommend lots of stock purchases or sales just to run up their fees.

A Registered Investment Adviser (RIA) has a certain level of training and must guarantee that recommendations and trades made for you are in your best interest. This is called fiduciary responsibility.

An RIA will probably be a bit more expensive, but you will have professional guidance from someone who has to have your best interests as their first responsibility.

A good RIA will make certain that you have a diverse portfolio that meets your needs and confidence levels. For instance, as a younger person, you may want a more aggressive portfolio that involves more risk but more potential gain. As you age, you will probably want to move your investments into a more secure portfolio.

Tax Consequences of Investing

Under taxes, I mention capital gains taxes. When you buy a stock, you have a basis. This is how much you paid for the stock. When you sell the stock, you either have a gain or a loss. If you sell the stock for more than you bought it for, you have a capital gain and must declare it on your taxes. If you sell the stock for less or the company fails, you have a capital loss. You can apply capital losses against taxes you may owe.

Always keep track of the basis! It will make figuring out your taxes much easier.

8. Retirement

You may feel like retirement is a long way away, but it will come faster than you realize. Planning ahead can make the difference between a retirement and working until you drop.

Setting up a retirement account usually involves a professional account manager or the Human Resources (HR) department at your work.

The earlier you start saving for retirement, the better off you will be. The graph below is what happens if you start a retirement account when you are 20 and put $1000 a year into it ($84 a month). If you average the low but safe 5% annual return each year until you retire, you will see some amazing returns. A 5% return means that for every dollar you invest, you get $0.05 a year - does not seem like much but it adds up. When you retire at 65, you will have $170,000. Your $45,000 has earned you $125,000

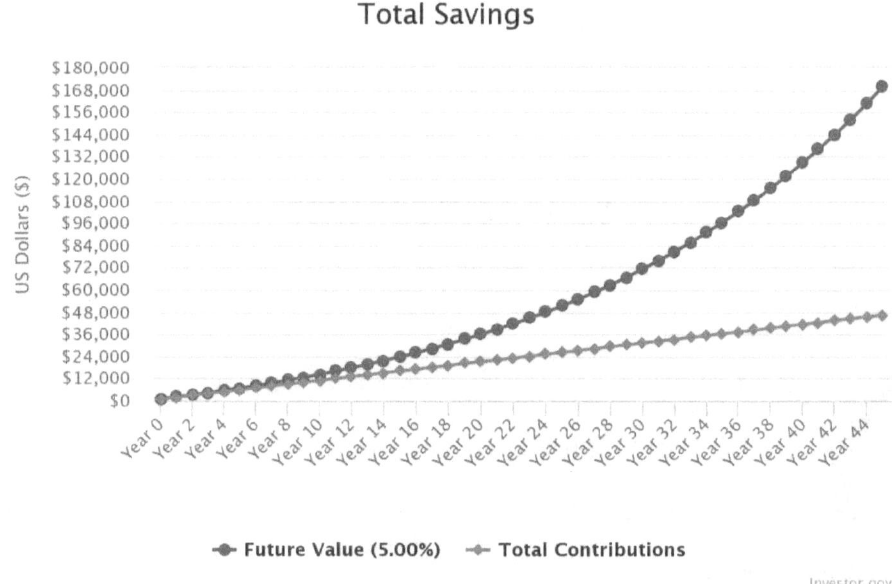

If you wait until you are 30 to start a retirement account and using the same $1000 a year and 5% return, you will deposit $20,000 and your retirement balance will be only $97,000 at age 65. That is not much.

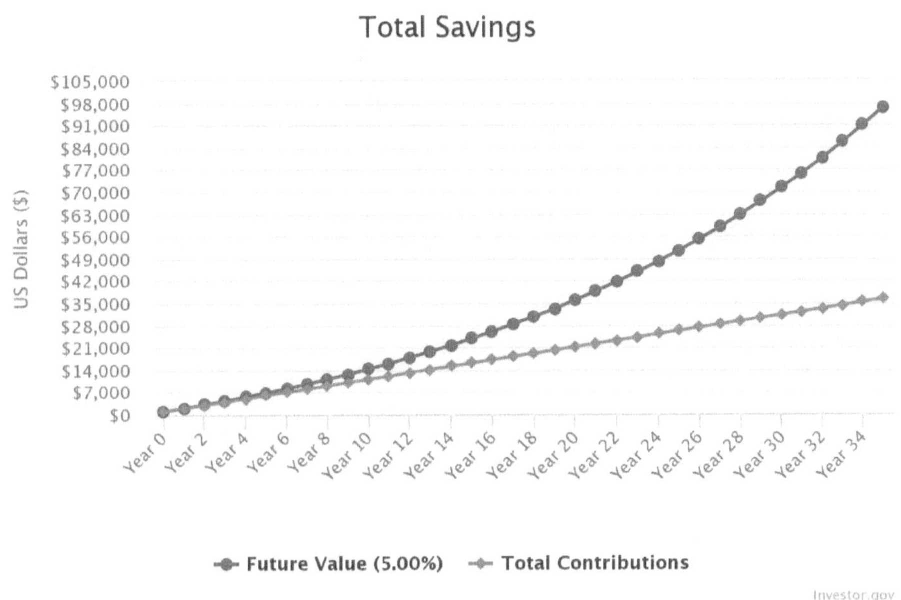

Retirement Accounts

According to the IRS, the following are all types of retirement accounts. Be aware that all of this is subject to change!

Social Security is paid to you by the federal government at retirement. (Remember those Social Security deductions from your paycheck?) Because Social Security may change by the time you are ready for it, we are not going to discuss it much. Do not expect Social Security to fund your retirement, it was never designed to do that. It is intended to supplement your retirement savings and to provide a safety net in case of bank failures like those of the Great Depression.

Roth IRAs

A Roth IRA (Individual Retirement Account) is set up through an investment broker. You can contribute as long as you or your joint filing spouse has taxable income. Your contribution (the money you contribute) is in after-tax dollars so you do not get a tax deduction, but you also do not pay taxes when you start getting distributions (money paid to you).

Traditional IRAs

The traditional IRA is also set up through a broker. Contributions are based on your income. Your contribution is in pre-tax dollars, so you get a deduction. However, you do pay taxes on your distributions.

With Roths, you pay taxes when you put the money in. In a traditional IRA, you pay taxes when you get the money out.

Employer Sponsored Retirement Plans

The names of these accounts represent the section of the IRS Code that defines them.

401(k) Plans

401(k) plans are provided by your employer. You have a portion of your pay deposited into the 401(k) and your employer may meet your contribution. You get a tax deduction when you put the money in and are taxed when you take it out. Always sign up for a 401(k). If you leave the company, you can roll (change) the 401(k) over to an IRA.

403(b) Plans

The 403(b) is similar to 401(k) but designed for public school employees and certain not-for-profit organizations.

SIMPLE IRA Plans (Savings Incentive Match Plans for Employees)

The SIMPLE IRA is an IRA that allow an employer to make contributions. These are often used by companies that do not offer 401(k) or 403(b) plans.

SEP Plans (Simplified Employee Pension)

For SEPs, you set up a traditional IRA and the employer contributes.

Payroll Deduction IRAs

Payroll deduction IRAs are Roth IRAs or traditional IRAs set up through a bank and funded with automatic payroll deductions.

Profit-Sharing Plans

Profit-sharing plans are distributions of profits made by the company. Profit-sharing is in addition to your wages/salary. Profits can vary wildly, and the company may choose to not make a distribution every year.

Defined Benefit Plans

Defined benefit plans are becoming rare. These provide a fixed, pre-established benefit established by the employer for employees at retirement.

Money Purchase Plans

Money purchase plans are similar to a 401(k) or 403(b), but there is a mandatory percentage contribution (such as 5% of your paycheck) to be matched by the employer.

Employee Stock Ownership Plans (ESOPs)

ESOPS are company stock issued to you. The value depends on the value of the stock when you retire.

Governmental Plans

This is the retirement fund for government (federal, state, tribal government) employees.

457 Retirement Plans

457s are available for certain state and local governments and non-governmental entities tax-exempt under IRC Section 501.

Setting Up a Retirement Account

If you are interested in an IRA or Roth IRA, contact a financial planner. Otherwise, you will go through your company's HR (Human Resources). Always take advantage of retirement accounts. You can have more than one.

You may need to be vested. This means you must stay at the company for a certain amount of time (twelve months, five years, ten years) in order for the retirement account to be activated. In some cases, if you are not vested, the company removes their contributions when you leave. In other cases, the retirement fund will be closed for you, and you will be responsible for taxes.

Retirement Goals

Your goal for retirement is 80% of your final pre-retirement salary times the number of years you plan to live after retirement (usually 20-30 years). That exact number can be a bit tenuous when you are just starting out.

Kiplinger, a personal finance media outlet, lists goals by age rather than percentages.

Age	Goal in terms of annual income
30	1/2 annual income
35	1 to 1 1/2 times
40	2 to 2 1/2 times
45	2 1/2 to 4 times
50	3 1/2 to 6 times
55	5 to 8 1/2 times

For example, if you are making $25,000 a year, you should have $12,500 in your retirement account at age 30.

The AARP (American Association of Retired Persons) offers a calculator to check retirement amounts based on your age, salary, and desired retirement lifestyle.

If you are behind in your goals, you can make efforts to make up the difference. Live within your means. That might mean taking fewer vacations, downsizing, and choosing not to spend money freely. Put any extra money into your retirement fund.

If you make your annual retirement savings goal, you can always use that extra money to fund an emergency account or other savings plan. If you have investments, hire a professional to make sure you are diversified and investing properly for your goals. Consider retiring later than earlier.

Always sign up for company-funded retirement accounts!

9. Taxes

You will be paying taxes in some form for the rest of your life. Let's look at the different types of taxes and then I will hit on state and federal income tax filings.

Types of Taxes

Sales Taxes

Sales taxes are set by states/counties and local governments to raise revenue (money) to run the city, county, and state. This is (partially) how your roads and schools are funded, and why you have free law enforcement and fire departments.

Sales taxes are charged on tangible (things you can touch) goods with the exception, in most states, of food purchased for in-home use. Sales taxes are collected by businesses and then remitted to the proper authority. Occasionally, the residents are asked to vote on special taxes that are used to support special projects.

Here are some examples: In Laramie, Wyoming, we have a 6% sales tax. That means if you buy a $1 candy bar, you pay $1.06. Four percent ($0.04) goes to the state. One percent ($0.01) goes to the county. The final 1% is called the 6th Cent Tax and is voted on every four years. The 6th cent income is used to support special projects.

If you were to buy the candy bar and a steak, you usually are not taxed for the steak, because you are going to add labor to the steak by cooking it at home.

When I lived in Alabama, we paid 11%, divided among the state, county, and city. This meant that if you purchased something in the city, you paid more than if you purchased the same item in the county, sometimes quite literally across the street!

Another example is when you have your car's oil changed. You will pay tax on tangible items like the oil and oil filter. You will not pay taxes on intangible items, like the mechanic's hourly wages.

Sin Taxes

Sin taxes are levied (charged) on luxury or dangerous goods such as luxury cars, cigarettes, and alcohol.

Travel Taxes

Travel taxes are levied on hotels, airports, and other travel-related locations. The base rate is set by the federal government, but counties and cities can add to that rate. For example, Albany County, Wyoming has a lodging tax of 4%. The 4% is on top of the 6% sales tax. This means that if you rent a hotel room in Albany County for $100 a night, you will pay 10% or $10. This lodging tax is used, in part, to promote tourism in Albany County.

Capital Gains Taxes

Capital gains taxes are levied on money that you make as passive income. Passive income means that you did not work for the money. A capital gains tax is levied when you sell the investment.

There are two types of capital gains taxes. If you buy and sell investments over a short period of time, you are taxed at your income tax rate. If you hold investments for a long period of time, the capital gains are taxed at a lower rate.

Capital gains taxes also occur when you sell real estate. For example, if you buy a house for $100,000 and sell it for $125,000, you have a capital gain of $25,000 and you, with some exceptions you do not need to worry about now, must pay taxes on it.

Inheritance or Estate Taxes

Inheritance taxes are levied when you get an inheritance (money or goods) after someone dies. Estate taxes are levied on the estate of the person who has died.

Income Tax

Income taxes are levied on anyone who receives a wage or salary. You have a tax rate that depends on how much money you make a year. This is a wildly complicated subject and income tax law is confusing and changes practically every year.

The short version is that you will pay a percentage of your income to the federal government and depending on your state, to your state, county and even city. You get to fill out an income tax form and send it plus possibly some money to the government on April 15 of each year. Sometimes you will get a refund from the government, which means that you have paid more taxes than you owe.

Payroll Taxes

If you remember the section on pay stubs, you had taxes withheld from your paycheck. These taxes include Medicare, Social Security Disability, Unemployment (worker's comp), and Social Security Retirement. Your state collects Medicare and Unemployment and distributes it on behalf of the federal government.

Property Tax

Property tax is levied on both real estate (land and houses) and on personal property (mobile homes, car registration, etc.). Both are levied by the county you live in.

Property tax is assessed by the county assessor and possibly the city assessor. Every year, you pay the county for any land or house or building you own. The collected taxes are used to support education, transportation, emergency services, parks, recreation, and libraries within the county or the city.

Personal property includes mobile homes, RVs, vehicles, boats, planes, ATVs, and other items that need to be registered or licensed. When you purchase a car, you are charged a sales tax on the car and then you pay an annual property tax when you purchase your license plate.

Filing Your Taxes

You will have to file your income taxes every year. The IRS has no sense of humor and no tolerance for people who avoid filing taxes. Yes, your money is generally misspent by the government. Vote for change instead of refusing to pay taxes.

I am going to assume you are single with no dependents and you do not own your own home. Otherwise, there are more documents you need! To file your taxes, you will need:

- Your social security number

- Identity Protection PIN, if one has been issued to you by the IRS

- Bank routing and bank account numbers to receive your refund by direct deposit

- Any communication from the IRS

- Any of the following forms (which are prepared for you and mailed to you or handed to you by your employer, after the end of the year) There are more than one type of each form and you may receive more than one form, but with a different letter designation, such as a W-2 and a W-2G.

  - IRS Notice 1444

  - Any W-2, 1099, 1095, 1098, 5498 form mailed to you

- In-kind (physical donations like clothing) or cash donations to a charity

- Itemized qualified educational expenses

- Vehicle sales tax paid and/or personal property tax

- Expenses related to investments

- Records of any scholarships or fellowships

- Amount of state and local income or sales tax paid (other than wage withholding)
- Jury duty records, hobby income and expenses, prizes and awards

Always keep those forms in a safe place. If you look under Records Retention, you will find hints for setting up a filing system and how long to keep your records. If you have a filing system you will find it far easier to file your taxes and, if you are audited by the IRS, to prove that you honestly filled out your taxes.

This is Financial Dragon's W2, based on his pay stubs. Yours will look like this, but with your own information. Compare it against your pay stubs to make sure it is correct.

22222	VOID ☐	a Employee's social security number	For Official Use Only ▶ OMB No. 1545-0008		
b Employer identification number (EIN)				1 Wages, tips, other compensation $20,800.00	2 Federal income tax withheld $860.00
c Employer's name, address, and ZIP code A Daley Book				3 Social security wages $20,800.00	4 Social security tax withheld $533.20
Laramie, Wyoming 82070				5 Medicare wages and tips $20,800.00	6 Medicare tax withheld $124.70
				7 Social security tips	8 Allocated tips
d Control number				9	10 Dependent care benefits
e Employee's first name and initial Financial	Last name Dragon		Suff.	11 Nonqualified plans	12a See instructions for box 12
Laramie, Wyoming				13 Statutory employee ☐ Retirement plan ☐ Third-party sick pay ☐	12b
				14 Other	12c
					12d
f Employee's address and ZIP code					
15 State WY Employer's state ID number	16 State wages, tips, etc. $20,800.00	17 State income tax $0.00	18 Local wages, tips, etc.	19 Local income tax	20 Locality name

Form **W-2** Wage and Tax Statement **2020**

Department of the Treasury—Internal Revenue Service
For Privacy Act and Paperwork Reduction Act Notice, see the separate instructions.

Copy A—For Social Security Administration. Send this entire page with Form W-3 to the Social Security Administration; photocopies are not acceptable.

Cat. No. 10134D

An audit is a formal investigation of your tax returns. You will have to prove that you indeed did make or spend or donate what you claimed you did. Any fees, interest, and penalties charged by the IRS for accidentally misfiling taxes can be unbelievably expensive and they are notoriously unforgiving. Fraudulently filing taxes can mean a lengthy jail sentence.

Should You File?

If you are under 19, your parents/guardian can claim you as a dependent. If you are a student, your parent/guardian can claim you as a dependent until you turn 24. Your tax status depends on which category you fall into and how much you make. If you have been filing under your parents' tax return, talk to a tax professional. It may be more advantageous for you to file as a single person.

If you make less than the minimum filing amount, consider filing a tax return anyway. The Earned Income Tax Credit (EITC) can return some of your taxes to you. If you are not sure if you qualify for the EITC, look on the IRS website for the EITC Assistant to see if you are eligible.

Students making less than the legal minimum can get deductions for higher education expenses and tax credits including the American Opportunity Credit.

Filling Out the Form

I would love to give a step-by-step primer on how to fill out the tax forms. However, the form is extremely unfriendly. The IRS does provide detailed instructions on which schedules you will need.

The IRS has several options to help you file your taxes. One is Free File, for which you are probably eligible. If your taxes are simple, look into VITA, the Volunteer Income Tax Assistant program. These trained volunteers will help you file your taxes for free. Both are recognized by the IRS, and you will find links on their website at irs.gov.

Be alert for scams and hustles. If you are offered a loan or advance on your tax refund, read the paperwork very carefully.

The RAL or Refund Anticipation Loan is a type of payday loan and often associated with very high-interest rates and fees. There is a very good chance that you will end up owing more on your loan than you received as a refund. In fact, the RALs are such a bad deal that the company that insures financial institutions (the FDIC) calls them unsafe and unsound.

Next Steps

In the next five sections, I will discuss topics that are more about understanding your financial situation and keeping you safe and organized. These sections include credit reports and credit scores, debt, credit cards, scams and data breaches, and records retention.

10. Debt

Debt is part of American life. Costs have risen substantially while wages have stagnated. We are also constantly sold a lifestyle of consumption through media and societal expectations. Do not let anyone separate you from your money without a really good reason! Remember, debt increases the cost (by way of interest charges) of whatever it is you are purchasing.

Debt by Age

Debt is money you borrow from a lender that allows you to purchase items. Each age group has a unique debt structure that reflects the needs and levels of importance placed on purchases.

Americans under 35 average about $67,400 in debt as of 2019. Of that, debt falls into two categories:

- 20% of that credit card debt (roughly $13,480)

- 21% represents student loans (roughly $14,154)

The under 35s also spend 40% of their monthly income on discretionary spending (stuff you do not need but want) or non-essential items like entertainment!

Americans between 35 and 44 average $133,100 in debt. Americans between 45 and 54 average $134,600. The general debt structure is:

- Mortgage debt

- Credit card debt

- Student loans

For the 55 to 64 age group, debt drops to $69,000 and continues to decrease. For all ages, credit card debt continues to be either the first or second cause of debt. For people over 75, workforce participation has increased because that age group generally has medical bills or was unable to plan for retirement.

Different Types of Debt

There are five different types of debt. Understanding those types can help you to understand what type of debt you may want to take out. The five categories are secured debt, unsecured debt, revolving debt, term loans, and mortgage. Debt can fit into more than one category.

Secured Debt

Secured debt is debt that is secured with an asset (item of value that you own) or collateral. For instance, the car is the collateral for your car loan. The asset or collateral can be seized if you fail to pay back the debt. Secured debt includes car loans, secured credit cards, and mortgages (which are a special type of secured debt).

Unsecured Debt

Unsecured debt has no collateral or asset backing it. If you do not repay the unsecured debt, you can be sued or sent to collections. Unsecured debt includes unsecured credit cards, membership contracts, and medical bills.

Revolving Debt

Revolving debt has a credit limit, and you can use up to that limit. As you repay the debt, you can spend up to the limit again. If you have a $5,000 limit, and you use $2,400, you have $2,600 that you can spend. Your repayment amounts vary based on how much of your limit you are using. Revolving debt can be secured (home equity line of credit) or unsecured (credit card).

Term Loans

Term loans are those that are paid off over a defined time frame. For instance, car loans are term loans. Your loan must be paid off in a certain number of months, commonly 24, 36, 48 or 60 months.

Mortgages

Mortgages are secured loans with real estate (a house or piece of land) acting as the collateral. Mortgages are considered a separate category because they are generally very long-term (15 to 30 years) and for large amounts of money. Mortgages are outside the scope of this book.

Interest Rates

When banks lend you money, they charge you interest. When they use your money through a savings account, they pay you interest. In this section, interest means you are paying the lender for using their money. You will find a worksheet on calculating interest at the end of the book.

There are two types of interest, simple and compound. Simple interest is figured by multiplying the daily interest rate by the principal times the number of days between payments.

Compound interest rates mean that you are paying (or earning) interest on the interest. If you carry a revolving balance on a credit card, your interest will be compounded.

Secured loans generally have better interest rates and terms than do unsecured loans. This is because there is something for the lender to seize. If you are using a piece of property or a vehicle as collateral and you sell it, you must repay the lender first out of the proceeds (lien).

Good Debt vs Bad Debt

Some debt types are considered "good" debt, while others are "bad" debt. Good debt involves buying items that increase in value after purchase. Bad debt involves buying anything that decreases in value as soon as you purchase it. Occasionally, there is a gray area where good debt becomes bad debt.

Examples of good debt include mortgages, home equity loans, student loans, and small business loans.

Examples of bad debt include clothing (yes, you need to wear clothing, but acquiring debt buying clothing is bad debt), appliances, entertainment, vehicles, credit card debt, and payday loans.

Examples of gray debt include mortgages, home equity loans, credit cards, student loans, and vehicles. Note that these may also be considered good or bad debt. Mortgages are gray because buying a house with mortgage payments that are more than you can afford puts you in danger of losing the house if the housing market crashes or you lose your job.

A home equity loan is borrowing against the equity in your home. Equity is what the house is worth, minus the amount of your mortgage. For instance, if you have a $100,000 house and owe $30,000, your equity is $70,000. Using a home equity loan to improve your financial situation by paying off high-interest credit card bills or making home improvements are good. These loans become bad when you make foolish home improvements or just run up your credit card debt again.

Credit cards are the most common type of debt for Americans. Credit cards make life much easier. The problem is that if you misuse credit cards, they become Bad Debt very quickly. Because credit cards are so important, I will discuss them in much greater detail under Credit Cards.

Education is great. Except when you take out a high-interest loan to attend an expensive school when a less expensive school will serve your educational needs. Another issue is to take out loans that are more than you will realistically expect to earn with that degree.

For instance, my middle child was considering art school. The art school they were interested in cost about $50,000 a year or $200,000 for four years. According to the US Department of Labor, the median annual wage for a multimedia artist is a cheerfully optimistic $75,270 a year. They would have to dedicate two or realistically three full years of income to pay back college expenses. Most people are not able to dedicate that kind of money to pay back their college expenditures and thus, student loans become a long-term responsibility and back breaker.

Buying an expensive vehicle (for your unique situation) is bad. Buying an appropriately priced car to help you get to work and school is a good debt. Thus, this is a grey debt.

Applying for Debt

When you decide to take out a loan or a credit card, the lender will look at several different factors. These are your credit report and credit score (see chapter 12), your debt-to-income ratio, and of course, your employment status. The better your credit score and the more secure your employment, the better the interest rate you will qualify for. Let's take a closer look at debt-to-income ratios.

Debt-to-income ratios (DTI) look at the total of all your debts divided by your gross monthly income. Once you multiply it by 100, you have a percentage. The lower your percentage, the better your DTI. To calculate debt to income ratio:

- Add up all your monthly debt payments (car loans, credit card minimum payments, etc.).
- Calculate your gross monthly income (what you make before taxes).

- Divide the debt by the income - this should give you a number less than 1. If it is greater than one, you have either made a mistake or you have more debt than income!

- Multiply that number by 100.

For instance: you have $1000 in monthly debt payments and $4000 in monthly income. The ratio is 0.25 or 25%.

A good debt-to-income ratio is less than 43%. The higher your debt-to-income ratio, the lower the statistical probability that you will be able to repay a new loan.

There is also a mortgage-to-income ratio that you will need to learn about when you start looking for a house and a mortgage.

Paying Down Debt

If you have gotten yourself into debt, now is the time to get out of debt! There are several ways to pay down your debt. It is very easy to get in debt, but it will take some work to get out of debt. Which method(s) you choose depends on your personality and unique situation.

The **Avalanche and the Snowball** methods were coined by Dave Ramsey, a financial adviser and author. In these, you pay off one bill and then take that money to pay off the next bill, etc. Here is an example: you have two credit cards with a balance on each. Decide which is the most expensive debt by looking at the annual percentage rate (APR) and your balances. You then choose either the smallest balance or the one with the highest APR to pay off first. You will put as much money as you can on the first debt while maintaining your minimum payment on the second one.

Once you pay off the first one, you take all that money plus the minimum payment you have been making and pay down the second card. If this sounds confusing, look in the Worksheets for practical help.

Paying off the highest APR card helps you eliminate finance charges. Paying off the lowest balance card first gives you a feeling of progress.

The **Balance Transfer** is a credit card that allows you to transfer all or most of your credit card debt onto one card with a 0% APR. Just read the fine print because the APR on balance transfers can be extremely high after the introductory period ends.

The **Personal Loan** involves finding a loan with a lower interest rate than your debts (also called streamlining or consolidation). You take the money from the lower interest loan to pay off higher interest rate loans. You then pay off the personal loan. To get the best interest, you need to have a good credit score.

Caution! If you obtain a debt consolidation loan, then get into more debt (say by using a credit card you just paid off), you are worse off than before. To make debt consolidation work requires the discipline to change spending habits and stay within your budget.

If you have acquired debt like a car loan, you may want to **refinance** it or take out a lower interest loan to repay the existing loan.

This is different from a personal loan because you are replacing an existing single loan with a new one. There are many refinance calculators online that can help you make an informed decision.

The bottom line is that you need to make a **budget**, regardless of your debt paydown strategy. If you know and control where your money is going, you stand a better chance of not getting into debt again.

Predatory and Unethical Lenders

A predatory lender is one who charges high-interest rates at unfavorable terms. If you have read any Charles Dickins, these were the usurers who caused so much heartache in his books. Take particular care when you are dealing with used car dealers. They have a negative reputation for a reason. Used car salespeople may ask what you can afford a month and then "make it happen" for you. You could end up with a loan that lasts for longer than the car does.

The value of the car decreases (depreciates) faster than the loan is paid off. Eventually, you will owe more on the car than the car is worth. You will not be able to sell the car and pay off the loan.

Before you look at a car, know what you are willing to pay, how much you can afford to pay, and how much the car is worth. Get the interest rate and length of time you will have the loan. Go home and work the numbers. If the seller tells you that there are other people who are ready to buy the car and you need to jump on it RIGHT NOW, walk away.

Payday loans and car title loans fall into the category of Do Not Ever Do This. These are extreme predatory loans. Payday loans are short-term loans against future earnings. A car title loan is a loan against the value of your car. You show a pay stub or car title to the payday lender, and they lend you what you can expect to make on the next payday or the value of your car. Both these loans come with extremely high-interest rates and finance charges. You may end up paying 400% in fees. This means for every $100 you borrow you repay $500! If you fail to repay your car title loan, you can lose your car.

Co-signing on a Loan

Co-signing means that you are responsible for someone's loan. This is a VERY BAD IDEA. All you need to do is tune into afternoon small claims court shows like *Judge Judy*. At least half of the cases revolve around co-signing.

Here's how co-signing works. Your friend or parent or significant other wants to get a new phone/car/etc. but their credit is not very good, or they do not have a job, etc. Your credit score is very good, so you agree to co-sign on the loan. Something happens - your friend loses their job, they do not want to be your friend anymore, you break up, whatever… Your friend stops paying the loan.

Guess who is responsible now? You are. If you fail to pay back the loan, your credit is ruined. You may not find out that the person is defaulting (not paying) on the loan until it is too late. You also have no legal right to get the car/phone/etc. back.

Only co-sign on a loan with someone who has the same attitude toward your finances that you have. In other words, if the other person is irresponsible with their money, why would you assume that they will be responsible with yours?

Debt After Death

Depending on what kind of debt you have when you die will determine what happens to it. There are different categories of debt; single debtor, co-signed, and JTWROS (pronounced joint-ten-ross) or Joint Tenants with Right of Survivorship. The court of law that "proves" your death will require that all debts be paid before any of your money or possessions can be handed out to your heirs (the people you are giving stuff to).

Single Debtor

If you have a debt that only has your name on it, your creditors will be notified by the person who is handling your legal matters (executor or personal representative). Creditors then have up to two years to make a claim against your estate - basically the money that is left after you die. If there is no money to pay them, the creditor cannot go after your heirs. The debt is erased.

DO NOT let a creditor tell you that you are responsible for your parents/significant other's debts. You are not responsible as long as your name is not on the debt! One big exception to this is if you live in a community property state (Arizona, California, Idaho, Louisiana, New Mexico, Nevada, Texas, Washington and Wisconsin and optionally in Alaska). Debts (and assets) are jointly owned by both spouses, regardless of the name on the paperwork. The other exception is for medical care under Medicare.

Co-signed Debt

If you have a co-signed debt, you and your co-signer are responsible for the debt. If your co-signer fails to pay the debt, you or your estate is now liable for the debt. In this situation, you may or may not get the co-signed item back.

For instance, you co-signed on a car loan, the car is totaled, and the other co-signer is killed. If they have the proper levels of insurance, the insurance company pays the creditor for the value of the car. If the co-signer took out a predatory loan, the value of the car versus the remaining debt on the car will not be equal. In this case, the insurance company pays the value of the car and you, the co-signer, is now liable for the remainder of the loan.

Joint Tenants with Right of Survivorship

Joint Tenants with Right of Survivorship means that two or more people hold property or bank accounts jointly. If one "tenant" dies, the other "tenant" immediately gets that property (and any debt associated with it) or access to money. Ownership of property does not have to be "proved" in a court which can take several months. It is generally used for real estate, property like cars, and investment accounts. There are some inheritance tax benefits to having property be JTENWROS.

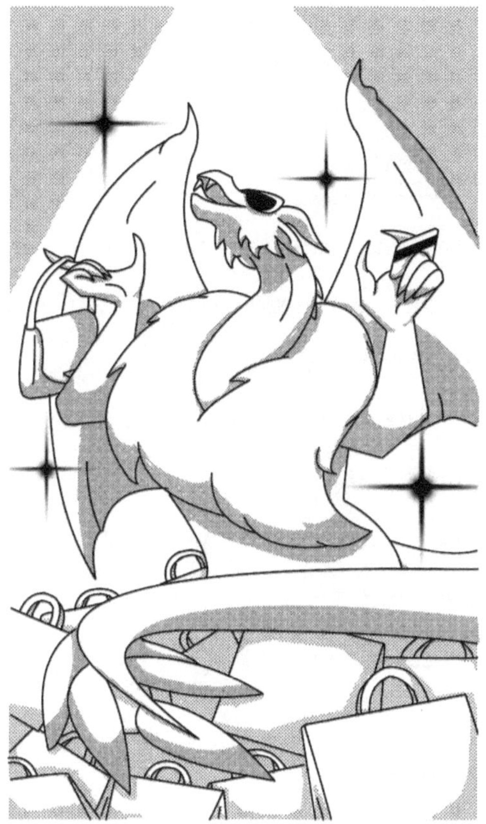

11. Credit Cards

Credit cards are a ubiquitous form of debt and are one of the easiest ways to get into debt but are almost a necessity for life. Credit cards will help you to build your credit. If you want to fly, rent a car, or stay in a hotel, you will need a credit card. They are far safer than debit cards to use on the internet.

They are also incredibly easy to abuse and are the number one cause of debt in the United States.

Credit Card Mechanics

Credit cards are revolving loans that can be secured or unsecured. In order to get a credit card, you need to choose which one you want and then apply for it. The lender will look at your credit score and history to determine your credit limit and your APR (interest rate).

All the following information, and much more, will be included in the fine print. Always read and understand the fine print. If you do not read and understand the fine print, you may have some very unpleasant discoveries when your bill arrives.

APR or Annual Percentage Rate

APR or Annual Percentage Rate is how much interest you pay over one year on any charges you do not pay off immediately. Your APR is based on the prime rate plus how much risk the lender feels it is taking in issuing your card. Prime rate is the base interest rate that can be charged and is set by the Federal Reserve. There are a number of APRs that can be applied to credit cards. These include:

Balance-transfer APR is applied to charges transferred from another card.

Purchase APR is charged on purchases.

Cash advance APR is charged on cash advances.

Introductory APR is an excellent interest rate charged for a limited introductory period.

Variable APR changes with the prime rate.

Fixed APR does not vary but can be changed by the lender with notification.

Penalty APR is a higher APR that you are charged if you miss a payment or make a late payment

Credit Limit

Your credit limit is how much you can "borrow" on your credit card. This is determined by your credit report. If you have a secured card, your credit limit is the amount of cash you have deposited with the credit card issuer. The credit limit may also be called line of credit, credit line, or spending limit.

Balance

The balance is how much of your credit limit you have used and how much is revolving. For instance, if you have charged $1,000 on your card and you pay off $400, your balance is $600.

Balance Transfer

This involves transferring balance on one card to another card to get a better interest rate.

Billing cycle

This is the amount of time between one statement closing date and the next closing date, usually 21 days.

Cash Advance

Cash advance is borrowing money from your credit card. This is very expensive because there is an extremely high APR and no grace period. Avoid cash advances.

Fees

Credit cards make a killing off their fees, and they have a huge variety. Not all cards have all the fees, but all of the cards have some fees! Here are a few of them.

Annual fees are charged for the privilege of using their card. Sometimes the annual fee comes with perks, but most of the time it is a waste of money.

Balance transfer fees are charged on balance transfers, usually 3%- 5%.

Cash-advance fees are 5% of cash advance or $10, whichever is greater.

Foreign transaction fees are charged on purchases made outside the US, usually 3% of charges.

Late payment fees are applied if you miss your payment date. You can be charged $29 for first-time instances and up to $40 for subsequent missed payments over the next 6 billing cycles.

Grace Period

The grace period is the amount of time between the end of the billing cycle and when your bill is due. No interest is charged on your balance in this time and must be at least 21 days. Grace periods do not apply to cash advances or balance transfers.

Minimum Payment

This is the smallest amount you must pay each month. It is either a percentage of your balance or $25, whichever is greater.

Credit Card Positives

Credit cards can be safer than cash or debit cards. If you lose cash or are robbed, that money is generally gone. If your debit card is hacked, your entire checking account balance can be emptied out. It is far harder to get back your money after debit card fraud occurs.

Credit cards come with protection against fraud (someone uses your card without permission). As long as you notify the card about the fraud, you are not liable for the charges. If you receive a call from the fraud department, hang up your phone and dial the number on the back of your credit card. Do not give your personal info just because someone "from your credit card" called you.

If you are in a dispute with a vendor, the credit card company will investigate and may reverse the charges. You will need to alert the credit card company and fill out their required forms.

Credit cards make travel easier. You will find car rentals, hotels, and airlines require credit cards. One reason, thanks to 9-11, is because they want to prove you are who you say you are and not a cash paying terrorist. Another is that hotels want a way to recoup stolen towels and room damage. They will take a debit card but will place a hold on some of the money in your account. It will be released in a few days, but in the meantime, you cannot access that money.

If you are traveling internationally, many countries will take credit cards but not debit cards. The exchange rate to change US dollars into the currency of the country you are in is often better when using a credit card.

Credit cards may come with perks like rental car insurance, travel insurance, and even product warranties. Check your card's perks to see what you are missing out on.

Credit cards help build credit when you use one responsibly and pay off balances on time. Credit cards are great in an emergency!

Credit Card Negatives

Interest rates are higher than other loans because credit cards are generally unsecured - there is nothing the lender can repossess to help pay off the debt.

Failing to pay off a credit card in full each month builds your debt quickly through interest rates and fees. Missing or skipping payments counts heavily against your credit.

Credit card terms can be hard to understand. The fine print is printed in a tiny hard-to-read font. If you skip the fine print, you may be unpleasantly surprised by the sudden increase in interest, penalties, and fees.

Credit card minimum payments allow you to pay off interest and penalties but do not decrease the principal very quickly.

Credit cards offer easy access to cash advances. Great when you need the cash, but then they levy a processing fee and stiff interest rate that begins the day you take out the money, not the due date.

Credit cards are an easy way to make up a shortfall in income. However, this leads very rapidly to a lot of debt.

Credit Card Companies

There are four major credit card companies in the United States, although there are dozens if not hundreds of card issuers. The credit card companies are Visa, Mastercard, American Express, and Discover. Which company you choose depends on your needs.

In general, American Express has higher annual fees and bigger perks than the other three. If you plan on a lot of international travel, AmEx is not your best choice, unless you are planning luxury travel.

Discover has some low rates and is recognized almost everywhere in the US but is not recognized internationally.

Visa and Mastercard are recognized almost everywhere in the world. They are solid, workhorse cards with a lot of options.

There are small cards that allow you to shop specific stores but are not useful outside that specific store. One example is Fingerhut credit cards which are only usable through their catalog.

When you apply for a card, you may have a different issuer - your college or your profession may offer cards. Chase, CapitalOne, Wells Fargo, and Citibank are some of the issuers. For instance, you may end up with a Chase Mastercard or a Citibank Visa card.

Each of these different issuers has dozens of cards with different interest rates, annual fees, rewards, etc. When you go to choose a card, make certain you understand all the options and what you are signing up for.

Types of Credit Cards

As you start looking for a credit card, you will find many different types from every issuer. Which one you pick will depend on your situation and what you want from your credit card.

Low Interest

Low interest credit cards have low annual interest rates (APR) or may offer a 0% APR promotion. You will not earn many perks like cash-back or air miles. The promotional APR may seem great, but the interest rates after the promotion ends may be higher than average.

Balance Transfer

Balance transfer credit cards allow you to transfer all or part of the balance of your other credit cards to a lower or 0% APR card for 6 to 21 months. There may be an upfront fee for the transfer. The APR after the introductory period can be very high.

Rewards or Cash-Back

Rewards or cash-back credit cards earn either rewards like magazine discounts, florist purchases, etc. or earn you a certain percentage of cash back on purchases. The cash-back can be offered on all purchases or on selected categories based on purchase type or monthly promotions. Use the cash-back to pay off your credit card (it is not much, but every penny helps!).

Travel

Travel credit cards earn air miles, hotel stays, and other travel perks. Many times, they are branded so you can only earn travel credits at a specific chain or airline.

Secured

Secured credit cards are great for building or rebuilding credit. You secure them with a cash deposit and that becomes your credit limit.

Student

Student credit cards are available for students and do not require a security deposit. Some come with perks and rewards.

Bad or Limited Credit

Unsecured credit cards for bad or limited credit are generally very expensive with outrageously high APR or fees. Limited credit means that you have not built up much of a credit report.

Store

Store credit cards are issued by a specific chain such as Target or Wal-Mart. They may have perks or earn you purchasing credit at that specific store. The interest rates are generally higher, and the credit limits are lower. Closed-loop cards are good only in that chain while an open-loop card allows you to use it anywhere.

Minimum Payment Trap

If you carry a balance on your credit card and only make the minimum payment, the truth is that you will never pay off your credit card. The minimum payment is usually a percentage of your balance (generally 1 to 3%) or $25, whichever is greater.

Your minimum payment is applied first to any penalties or interest that you have accrued. The rest, whatever is left, is applied to your balance.

Your credit card statement tells you how long it will take to pay off your card making only minimum payments. This assumes that you never use your card again. Let's look at what happens when you have an average credit card and make only minimum payments.

- Credit card balance: $5,000
- APR: 21.21%
- Minimum payment: 2% or roughly $100
- Time to pay off: 10 years
- Finance charges: $7,282.74
- Total paid: $12,282.72

Now, let's add $25 to your minimum payment.

- Credit card balance: $5,000
- APR: 21.21%
- Monthly payment: $125
- Time to pay off: 6 years
- Finance charges: $3,757.13
- Total paid: $8,758.13

As you can see, that little extra saves you a huge amount in finance charges and how long you will be paying off your bill.

If you can make a minimum payment each month and a bit more each week, you can make amazing headway on paying down your credit card bill. The first payment goes towards penalties and interest charges, but the weekly payments pay down the balance.

12. Credit Reports and Credit Scores

If you are interested in getting loans or credit cards, you need to have a credit score and a credit report. The better your credit score is, the better terms and interest rates you will be able to get.

The credit report and credit score are not measures of how well you are doing financially. The report and the score are merely measures of how good you are at paying your bills and what kind of money lending risk you are.

Credit Reports

The credit report is a look at your spending and repayment habits. There are three main credit reporting agencies: Experian, Transunion, and Equifax. If you apply for a job, rent an apartment, or apply for a loan, you most likely will have a credit report "pulled" or released to the requester. A poor credit report indicates that you are a bad risk for employment, repayment, or rental.

Your report will show:

- Your credit score
- A list of everyone to whom you owe money
- All open accounts
- All closed accounts
- All defaults (you did not pay back the loan)
- All bankruptcies
- Any inquiries about your credit

Most data stay on your credit report for seven years, but serious issues like bankruptcies may stay on as long as ten years. Mistakes can and do happen. I will discuss those and what to do about them in a later section.

Credit Scores

Once you have a credit report, a company called FICO or more recently, another called VantageScore, scores your data. FICO and VantageScore are data analytic companies. Before FICO, you had to know someone, or have a lot of collateral, or pay outrageous interest rates to get a loan. The credit score process changed that and allowed people to get loans based on their history of paying back loans. FICO and VantageScore rate your information a bit differently, but they are very consistent with each other.

There are a number of factors that affect your credit score. These are length of credit history, payment history, credit utilization ratio, credit mix, and recent applications.

Length of Credit History

This is important to see trends. In order to have a FICO score, you need at least six months of reporting. The older your credit history is, the better your score.

Payment History

Payment history is one of the two MOST IMPORTANT factors in your credit score. This single factor counts for 35% of your score. If you have a series of late or missing payments, your score will be lower.

Always make your payments on time. If you cannot make payments on time, contact your lenders and see if you can adjust the payment dates to better correspond with your paydays. Always get that date change in writing.

Credit Utilization Ratio

This ratio is the second-highest ranked data in your credit score. This number looks at how much debt you have compared to how much revolving credit you have. You want to have a credit utilization ratio of 30% or less. It is not as confusing as you may think.

1.   Figure out how much credit (your credit limit) you have on your credit cards and other revolving loans

2.   Figure out how much debt (what you owe) you have on those revolving loans

3.   Divide the debt amount by the credit amount

4.   Multiply that by 100

If your credit utilization score is higher than 30%, concentrate on paying down your credit cards and not using them. If you have unused credit cards, do not worry about closing them. Their appearance on your credit history will improve it through credit utilization.

Credit Mix

Lenders like to see that you have revolving loans, mortgages, car loans, etc. on your report. This is tough to do when you are just starting out. If you rent, you can pay for a rent reporting service that will add your payments to your credit report. Alternatively, you can report rent to Experian Boost which will improve your Experian score but not Transunion or Equifax.

Another option is to take out a small loan and put all the money into a savings account. Pay back the loan using that money over time. I cannot stress it enough - pay your bills on time.

Recent Applications

Each time you apply for a loan or a credit card, the lender will conduct a "hard pull" on your report. This means that your entire credit report will be released to the lender. Every hard pull causes a short-term decrease in your credit score. There are also "soft pulls" that release a limited credit report to potential employers, landlords, or for pre-screening loans. These soft pulls do not affect your score.

The hard pulls lower your credit in the short-term because it signals that there are changes in your financial future. You may want a new credit card to make up short falls in income which means that your ability to repay debt is decreased.

Do not apply for every credit card you are offered, especially at big box stores. In addition, contact the three companies and place a freeze on your credit history. This means that no one can do a hard pull without your express permission.

Your First Credit Score

If you have just reached the six-month requirement for reporting and want to check your credit score, you can expect to see a score between 500 and 700. Since your payment history is the first most important factor in determining credit scores, your first credit score will be based on how well you did paying your bills. The second factor is credit utilization. If you have kept your credit utilization score below 30%, you should be in good shape.

If your first credit score is low, evaluate how you are managing your credit cards and other debts. A poor first-time credit score could indicate some financial problems in your future!

FICO and VantageScores

Your credit score ranges from 300 to 850. Scores above 650 are considered good credit scores.

FICO credit scores	VantageScores
Exceptional 800-850	Excellent 781-850
Very Good 740-799	Good 661-780
Good 670-739	Fair 601-660
Fair 580-669	Poor 500-600
Very Poor 300-579	Very Poor 300-499

If you have a low credit score and want to improve it, do not fall for promises made by overnight credit improvement companies. There are two factors that you must improve to improve your score: payment history and credit utilization ratio, and those companies cannot help you to raise those. Save your money and pay your bills on time and pay your revolving loans down.

Managing Your Credit Report

You are legally entitled to one free credit report a year from the big three agencies. In order to maximize their usefulness, request from one company in January, request from one company in May, and one from the final company in September, and then repeat each year. The companies do not share data among themselves, so you need to keep an eye on all three. To get your free report, contact:

- TransUnion https://www.transunion.com/

- Experian https://www.experian.com/

- Equifax https://www.equifax.com/personal/

Once you get the report, examine it carefully. If you find any errors, immediately contact the company in writing. You can clear up errors, but it will take time and perseverance.

To fix errors, write a letter explaining the error and send a copy of the report with the error highlighted via a certified letter (go to the post office and they will help you). Ask them to remove the error and send you a corrected copy of your report. Keep a copy of your letters to the credit reporting company. If they request more information, send it to them promptly. You may need to follow up.

To remove unauthorized credit inquiries, you will follow the same basic format. You must authorize a company to hard pull your credit report. If you did not give permission, tell the credit reporting company. And of course, follow up.

Credit Score Apps

In addition to requesting your annual free report, consider signing up for a credit monitoring app. Many people discover that they have been victims of identity theft by checking their credit report.

Mint is also a budgeting app, so if you have Mint already, you can keep an eye on your VantageScore from Experian.

Credit Karma offers both an app and a website. You will get FICO scores based on TransUnion and Equifax as well as credit card utilization and payment history. Credit Karma is simple to use and sends emails if reports change.

13. Scams and Data Breaches

Most people who have grown up with internet access probably have a better grasp about the types of online scams than do older generations. I will hit on the basic types of scams and then go deeper into what to do if you are part of a data breach and ways to protect yourself against hacking and scams.

Types of Scams

No matter what type of social media you are on, there are also scammers. When you set up your account, always use a strong password. Many sites offer two-step verification processes. Take advantage of those, even if they are annoying.

Make certain you are on the verified site before you log in and use https to log in. As you use a social media site, be suspicious. Why is that celebrity following you? Is it really a celebrity? Do not click on suspicious links in Facebook, Twitter, emails, etc.

The more urgent the message from a company or random communicator, the higher the probability the opportunity being offered is a scam. Remember the old saying, "If it sounds too good to be true, it is." If the deal is unreal, do some comparison shopping and check out the shipping costs while you are looking.

It is very easy to set up a website that looks just like the original. If you are not certain the website is legit, do a search and then compare the verified one (and their email address) to what you received.

Do not respond to requests for personal information (known as phishing). The IRS, police department, sheriff department, etc., will not contact you via phone, social media, or email. You will get a formal letter, or they will visit you in person.

Do not give away passwords, social security number, address, voter affiliation, etc. without thinking about WHY the requestor needs it. Likewise, do not enter your credit card or debit card unless you have verified the webpage!

Safer Shopping Online

Use your credit card for online shopping. Your debit card can be hacked, and you can lose all the money in your account before you realize it. Since most credit cards come with fraud protection and additional warranties, using one to shop online makes more sense.

If you do use your debit card, set a daily spending limit through your bank to keep from losing more than you can afford.

Always look at your credit card statement and dispute odd charges. Hackers may make small charges and if you do not notice them, they will begin to charge more and more.

Prepaid credit cards are a great online shopping idea. You can only spend what is on the card and thus hackers cannot make charges for expensive items.

Check the country of origin before you buy. I once bought an electrical item from a website that turned out to be in Australia. Not only would it not work in the US, but when I returned it, it vanished when it got to Australian customs, and I lost the money. In addition, CDs/DVDs from other countries may not play on American machines.

Data Breaches

Data breaches happen every single day and all that data becomes fair game on the Dark Web. One 2019 breach released 2.7 billion identity records, 774 million email addresses, and 21 million passwords. All this data was posted for sale. If you have not been in a data breach, you will be.

Take a few minutes to set up the following security steps:

A credit freeze restricts access so that most lenders cannot see your credit report until you unfreeze it with a PIN (Personal Identification Number). A freeze will prevent thieves and hackers from taking out loans and credit cards in your name. Generally, a credit freeze is free and simple to set up with Experian, TransUnion, and Equifax. Just do not lose that PIN number!

A credit lock is similar but can be unlocked via your phone or computer with a phone call. Locks are generally not free and come with some sort of monthly fees.

Set a daily spending limit on your debit card. Mine is set at $500 which means I cannot spend more than $500 in any one day using the debit card. Having a limit will prevent a hacker from stealing more than your daily spending limit. This can be temporarily lifted with a phone call to the credit union.

Change passwords once a year and set up difficult passwords. Generate safe and difficult passwords using a password generator and then store your passwords on a site like LastPass or Dashlane.

Monitor your credit. I discussed this under the credit section, so review that for the how-tos.

Check your email addresses on haveibeenpwned.com. This website tracks if your email address(es) has been compromised and will give you suggestions on what was released, and which websites were breached.

A recent search of my commonly used email address showed that my email addresses, password hints, passwords, and usernames have been released in a number of data breaches. My breaches included Adobe, CafePress, LinkedIn, MySpace, Chegg, My FitnessPal, and ShareThis. In addition, my email showed up in breaches of breaches including Antipublic Combo List, Collection 1, Data Enrichment Exposure from PDL Customer, exploit.in, Pemiblank, River City Media Spam List, and verifications.io. Where these data breaches first originated is generally not known. Change your passwords immediately!

Practice cybersecurity by not clicking on links or opening attachments in emails. If you know the sender but the link does not seem like anything the sender would send, think before opening it!

Do not respond to texts or emails from government agencies, alerts that your PayPal account has been suspended unless you click here immediately, or other attempts to get you to open a link.

If possible, always use two-factor authentication to log into accounts.

If you are notified of a data breach, keep a record of what you do in response. Document that you changed your passwords, placed a credit freeze, closed a credit or debit card, etc.

Experts recommend having an email for traveling and reservations, another for bills, and another for logging into websites. By doing this, you create another layer of cover between your primary email and information and your online activities.

Types of Data Breaches

Experts list five different types of data breaches: healthcare, financial, government, education, and entertainment. Healthcare often involves someone trying to get medical care by pretending to be you. Financial is your banking information. Government involves the IRS and any other federal agency for whom you may have worked or do business with. Education is, again, pretending to be you to get loans, etc. And entertainment involves activities like people hacking your video game information or getting data through ticket venues.

If you have suffered a data breach, here is a quick guide to what to do next. First, confirm that there was a data breach by calling the company. An email could be a phishing scam. Next, find out what data was stolen. Accept the company's offers to help to get any damage repaired and protect personal information. Finally, change passwords, logins, and security questions and answers.

14. Record Retention

Some of your records must be kept for legal purposes. The IRS can audit for good faith errors (unintentional mistakes) up to three years, and six years if they think you have underreported your income, or unlimited if investigating fraud. If you have the records, it is easier to defend yourself. If you set up a filing system for your papers, life will be much simpler!

Organizing Your Files

Your first step is to get organized. The easiest way I can suggest for tracking records is to buy a three-drawer filing cabinet or filing boxes and a stack of file folders. In the Worksheet section, I break down how you will use each box, what goes in the files, and how long you need to keep each record. Obviously, if you have a filing system that works for you, use that one.

Make one of your New Year's projects cleaning out the Shred box/drawer. Pay to have the paperwork shredded, get a crosscut shredder, burn the papers – just do not throw them away in the garbage! It is worth your money to protect yourself from identity theft.

Storing Personal Paperwork

You will need one more box for storing important personal paperwork. This box should either be a fireproof box or a safe deposit box since the papers stored in these are extremely important.

A safe deposit box is held at a bank or credit union. They are very secure - the box is locked within a locked vault and there is generally a two- or three-step identity verification process for the tenant. They are not stored in your house, so they are safe from natural disasters - although not from damage to the bank. On the negative side, they are only accessible when the building is open, and the contents are not insured against damage. If what you are storing in there is irreplaceable, you need to have some insurance for the items. In addition, you must pay an annual fee for the box.

Fireproof and waterproof safes have several great attributes. On the plus side, fireproof safes are not that expensive. You can also access it at any time. However, they are portable, so they can be easily stolen. A fireproof safe means the papers will not burn, but they can be heat damaged or destroyed. The safes may also be lost in tornadoes/ hurricanes or floods. Fireproof/waterproof boxes can develop a humidity problem. I discovered this the hard way when my middle child's passport molded while in their fireproof box.

Store the following in your fireproof box or safe deposit box:
Originals of:
- Birth certificates
- Marriage certificates
- Divorce papers
- Insurance papers
- Adoption records
- Death certificates

Copies of
- Living will/ health directive
- Wills
- Powers of attorney
- Front page of passports
- Credit card back and front

And the following
- Deeds or title to any property
- Car titles and extra car keys
- Paper copies or digital copies of family photos
- Written and photo inventory of household goods for insurance replacement

- Passport
- Social Security cards
- Credit cards you do not use

Items heirs and family members need in an emergency including
- Your attorney's name and phone number
- Information about debts (lender name, amount owed, monthly payments, due dates, etc.)
- List of current passwords
- List of doctors and any medications

DO NOT store original wills, living wills/health directives or powers of attorney in your fireproof box. The originals should be at your lawyer's office. If you create a will using NoLo (no lawyer) paperwork (available online), you will have to store the originals in your fireproof box.

15. Legal Stuff

As soon as you turn 18, the law views you as an adult and no one can have access to your information unless you give them permission. The main issue is if you are incapacitated or die, you have no one to speak for you. The law has several documents that you can use to allow someone else to speak on your behalf.

Throughout this book, I have suggested talking with a lawyer. Lawyers are expensive; however, your state university may have a law school that offers pro bono (free) or sliding scale legal services. Student lawyers gain experience by practicing law under the supervision of their qualified instructors. It is a great solution for simple legal issues.

Power of Attorney

A power of attorney gives the person you name all rights and power to conduct business in your name. If you give someone a full power of attorney, that person can take out loans in your name, sell your assets, empty out your bank account, and more.

DO NOT give anyone a complete power of attorney unless 1) you trust them implicitly, and 2) you have thought long and hard about giving them that much power over your life.

There are many types of powers of attorney that give another person a limited ability to conduct business on your behalf. For instance, there is a Limited Power of Attorney for Health Care which kicks in if you are incapacitated and need someone to make medical decisions for you. You can get a Limited Power of Attorney to sell a specific vehicle that you do not own or to allow someone to conduct limited business in your name.

You can always change the person you have named. You need to know the person you name very well, and they must understand your wishes.

If you are in a non-traditional relationship and you want your partner to make healthcare decisions for you, talk to doctors, and to even be allowed to visit you in the hospital, you need some sort of power of attorney. Otherwise, parents or siblings can cut you or your partner out of the decision processes.

Living Will/Advanced Directive

A living will is a guide to the medical decisions that you want made for you. If you do not want heroic measures, you can state the level you want. You can decide if you want to be an organ donor or have blood transfusions. The living will is not a binding document and can be disputed, but at least your wishes are stated, and your representative has proof to fight for your medical care while you are incapacitated.

There are a number of questions in the Worksheet section that you may want to consider when writing a living will. Your lawyer will have others.

Will

Once you start acquiring assets and dependents, you need to have a will. A will does not mean you are going to die; it means you are being a responsible adult. Despite what the movies may have you believe; you cannot make unreasonable requests like "divorce your wife or you do not inherit."

If you die without a will (intestate), your assets are divided depending on a formula set by the state.

A will is a statement of how you want your assets distributed and who will be your Executor or Personal Representative. This is the person who makes certain that your will is executed. You can give your assets to certain people, provide for your dependents including who will care for them.

A will does not have to be fancy. You can write one on a napkin and have it witnessed (signed) by two other people. It helps to have it notarized, but that is not necessary.

Estate

An estate is a fancy will for people with more assets.

Intestate

To die intestate means that you died without a will. This makes it difficult for your loved ones and may tie your assets up in court for years.

Probate

Probate is what happens when your will is proven in court. This process makes the will or estate a valid document. Your debts will be paid, your assets distributed, and your final wishes for interment carried out.

Retainer

A retainer is an amount of money that you pay a lawyer to work for you. Not all lawyers require a retainer, but some will ask you to pay a certain amount of money and then will do that much in legal work for you.

Death

Most of us have no idea how the legal system works after someone dies. We learn it the hard way and it is very bewildering at a time when you are already shaken and hurting. Depending on why your loved one died, you may be introduced to probate court, criminal court, civil court, and insurance companies all at once.

Probate court proves wills. Criminal court prosecutes crimes. Civil court handles cases that did not violate a law. In this case, the death might be from medical malpractice. It does help to have a guide, like a lawyer, to help you through all this.

Here are the basics for proving a will. You will need:

A death certificate issued by the coroner where the death occurred.

The most current version of the will or estate of the person who died. Hopefully, it is at their lawyer's office, and you know who their lawyer is.

In the will, someone is named as Personal Representative (PR) or Executor. This person will handle all the legal paperwork for the deceased person.

The PR will file a petition in probate court asking to be formally appointed to act on behalf of the estate. If there is no named PR or no will at all, you file a petition to notify all possible heirs and ask to be named the PR.

The PR identifies all assets and provides a valuation for them. Assets include real estate, vehicles, investments, bank accounts, cash, personal property, intellectual property (like copyrights and patents), and pets.

The PR notifies all creditors of the death. The probate court will get a record of all creditors and the amount owed. You need to publish a notice in the legal section of the dead person's local newspaper as well.

The PR then pays off all pre-existing debts like utility bills, mortgages, etc. If there is not enough cash, the PR must sell assets to raise the money.

The PR makes and pays for funeral arrangements. If there are reasonable preferences stated in the will, the will must be followed.

The PR must file two sets of tax returns for the dead person. One is for time in the current tax year that the person was alive. The second is for the person's estate.

The final step is to distribute the assets or what is left of them. If there is a will, the assets are distributed according to the will. It can be extremely specific, such as "the Ford Taurus goes to my second daughter" or as vague as "divide it all equally and give an equal amount to each heir."

If there is no will, the assets are divided according to a formula set by the state. In general, your legal spouse gets a percentage, then children, then siblings and so on. In some intestate proceedings, the fourth cousin six times removed who has no idea who you are must be tracked down and have assets from this stranger land on them (along with all the taxes).

Here are my takeaways on death and wills. Some of this was from personal experience and some from friends' experiences.

Choose your personal representative carefully. This is a huge job and requires a lot of attention to detail. If your possible PRs are not up to the task, ask a good, qualified attorney to serve.

Write your will carefully. Families have been destroyed by greed and selfishness. If your heirs are known to be difficult, spell out your wishes in detail.

Do not use your will as a threat. Write it, review it once a year, and live (or die) with your decisions. My attorney has a client who changes her will every few months in order to keep her children in line. If she is temporarily displeased with one child, changes her will, and then dies, that child must either hope their siblings share or dispute the will in court.

The concept of death is frightening, and no one wants to discuss final plans. However, preparing for the end is possibly one of the most adult actions you can take.

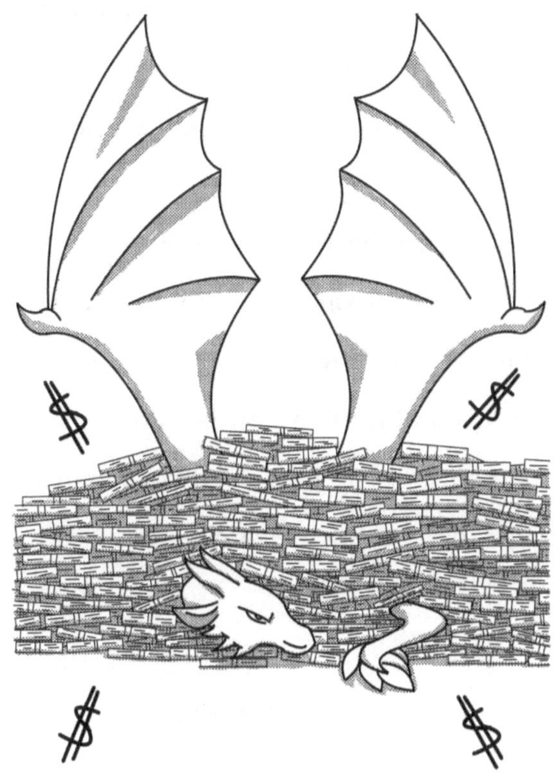

Final Words

A dulting is hard work and managing money is part of what makes adulting hard. If you spend a bit of time each week or day focusing on your money, where it is going, and on your decision making, you will find that it not only gets simpler, but you will reap rewards in terms of not taking on too much debt.

Investing is something that you should do. It is not only for the wealthy. Investing is a way to make your money work for you and can help you to retire in comfort or at least without food and shelter concerns.

And finally, learning to manage money will do a lot for your relationships. The number one cause for fights between partners is money - how it is spent and by whom.

I am not advocating that you become a hoarder and a miser, living a life without joy or the occasional latte. I am advocating for you NOT to end up eating nothing but ramen noodles for two weeks every month!

Happy adulting!

Worksheets

Budgeting

I am going to lay out the budget for a 50/30/20 budget. If you do not want to use it, that is fine. You'll use the same data for any budget you want to use.

Income	monthly	annual
Net paycheck		
Other income		
Total		
50% needs (multiply total by 0.5)		
30% wants (multiply total by 0.3)		
20% savings (multiply total by 0.2)		

If you live somewhere particularly expensive, you may need to adjust the 50/30/20 to reflect that. For instance, you might need 60/30/10.

Next, keep track of all your expenses for at least a month. Fill out the needs form. Keep in mind that this budget is not exhaustive, and you can add in your specific needs. You will have different needs. Make sure you are including NEEDS – these are items that make life possible. I included internet because we have discovered in 2020 that internet is necessary!

Needs	monthly	annual
housing (rent)		
gas		
electricity		
water		
sewer/other		
internet		
car payments		
car insurance		
gas/fuel		
groceries		
prescription medications		
minimum debt payments		
minimum clothing purchase		
cellphone service		
health insurance		
Total		

Does the total match the 50% goal? If it does, hurrah! If it doesn't, what expenses can you adjust to drop the total to match your desired needs amount.

Use the following table to track your Wants. Obviously, this list is highly subjective. If this were mine, there would be a lot of expenses related to my horse like lessons for us.

Wants	monthly	annual
streaming services		
dining out		
memberships (gym, etc.)		
cosmetics		
salon services		

Does the total match the 30% goal? If it does, you are kicking butt and taking names. If it does not, what expenses can you adjust to drop the total to match your desired wants amount?

Keep in mind that this is not a forever budget. You adjust the numbers and figures as your life changes.

Now it is time to work on the Savings portion. I've included a section on Annual Set Aside because these expenses can be fairly large and hard to budget for on a monthly basis. Again, this is not exhaustive.

Annual Set Aside	monthly	annual
car insurance if annual		
car maintenance		
health insurance if annual		
licenses		
car tags/stickers		
annual subscriptions		
Total		

Divide by 12 for the monthly amount you need to set aside for make your annual expenses.

And finally, the 20% savings part. I would fill in the annual set aside amount first, then divide between the general and emergency savings until you have reached your first goal for the emergency – usually $1000.

Savings	monthly	current balance	goal
general			
emergency			
private retirement			
future purchases			
annual set aside			
debt payoff			
Total			

Copy these pages, make your own spreadsheets or find your own method of tracking expenses. The most important part is that you budget!

Calculating Interest Rates

Remember those algebra classes you swore you would never use? Get ready for Simple Interest!

Simple Interest is where you earn or are charged interest based on your principal. These include loans like mortgages and student loans.

Here's the formula: $A = P(1 + rt)$

P is your principal amount (that's how much you took out for the loan).
        Write it down here: P=__________

t is the time period in years or months. 12 months = 1 year. 24 months = 2 years. If your loan is in years, multiply the years by 12 to get months. If your loan is in months, divide by 12 to get years. You'll usually use months.
        Write down the time period here: t=________

r is the interest rate in decimal form. To get a decimal from a percentage, write down the percentage here_____. If it is a round number like 16%, put the decimal point at the end. Move the decimal two places to the left (0.16). If there is already a decimal point (16.5%), move the decimal two places to the left (0.165). This is your "r."
        Write r down here: r=________
Now fill in the blanks.
A= P_______ times (1 + r_____ times t_______)
Multiply r and t, fill in the blank below
A= P_______ times (1 + rt_______)
Add 1 to the sum of rt. Fill in the blank below.

A= P_______ times (1+rt_______)

Multiply P times the value you just wrote down. Write it down here.

A=_________

A is how much you will pay in interest over that time period.

Now…. For an example because I could never grasp the written version in math class.

P= $5000

t = 5 years (60 months)

r = 10% or 0.10

A = $5000 * (1+ 5 times 0.01)

A = $5000 * (1+ 0.5)

A = $5000 * (1.05)

A= $2500

You will pay $2500 in interest over five years. On this loan example, you will pay a total of $7500. This is the original $5000 plus $2500 in interest.

Compound Interest is when you are charged or earn interest on the principal and the interest. Credit cards and savings accounts use compounded interest.

Here's the formula: P (1 + r/n)^(nt)

And here's how to do it… find a compounding calculator online.

Debt to Income Ratio

Debt-to-income ratios look at the total of all your debts divided by your gross monthly income. A good debt-to-income ratio is less than 43%.

Add up all your monthly debt payments. Write that number here:____

Calculate your gross (before taxes) monthly income. Write that number here:________

Fill in these blanks: <u>debt</u>   ______
                         income______

Divide debt by income. Write this number here:______
Your number should be less than one.

Multiply that number by 100 to get a percentage (or move the decimal two places to the right):________

A good debt-to-income ratio is less than 43%.

And the example.
Debt $<u>1000</u> = 0.25
Income $4000

0.25 * 100 = 25%.

Paying Down Debt

As I discussed in the section on paying down debt, there are five methods to paying down debt. If you have debt, let's take a closer making your choices. All of these assume you stop running up debt.

First, write down all debts, minimum payments, and APR.

Debt Name	Debt Amount	Minimum	APR

Minimum payments – find a minimum payment calculator and feed the data above into it and fill out the table.

Debt Name	Interest payments	Total payments	Time to pay off

Avalanche payments – order your debt by highest to lowest APR and locate an avalanche calculator. Feed in the data and you'll get the following:

Interest payments	Total payments	Time to pay off

Snowball payments – order debts by smallest amount to largest and find a snowball calculator. Feed in the data and you'll get the following:

Interest payments	Total payments	Time to pay off

Personal Loan - find a payoff calculator and assume that you will put in the total amount of minimum payments you are making now. Fill in the blanks.

Amount of loan plus fees	
APR	
Interest payments	
Total payments	
Time to pay off	

0% Balance Transfer –you may not be able to transfer all credit cards onto this card and there will be fees, so figure those into your equation. Use the introductory time limit to figure out how much to pay. Take your total amount and divide by the number of months.

Amount of loan plus fees	
APR	
Interest payments	
Total payments	
Time to pay off	

Now that you have all the numbers, you can make an informed decision that will help you pay off your debt as fast as possible and save as much money as possible.

Choosing a Credit Card

The following is a decision tree. If you have not used a decision tree before, they are fairly simple. Just answer each question and go to whichever question your answers suggest. It is sort of like a flow chart. Obviously, your decision is up to you. This is just a way to clarify your choices. Use the questions below each Yes/No answer to help guide your choice of card.

1)   Do you have good credit?
   a) No – look for a student, bad or limited credit, or
       secured credit card
   b) Yes - go to question 2
2)   Are you planning a balance transfer but NOT use the card for purchases?
   a) No – go to question 3
   b) Yes – look for a 0% balance transfer card
       i)   How long does 0% APR term last?
       ii)   How much can you transfer?
       iii)   What fees are included?
       iv)   Are there any annual fees?
3)   Are you planning a balance transfer AND use the card for purchases?
   a) No – go to question 4
   b) Yes – look for a 0% balance transfer card
       i)   How long does 0% APR term last?
       ii)   How much can you transfer?
       iii)   What fees are included?
       iv)   Are there any annual fees?
       v)   What is purchase/post-introductory APR?
4)   Are you getting the card to make several one-time large purchases?
   a) No – go to question 5
   b) Yes – 0% introductory APR card

      i)   How long does 0% APR term last?
      ii)   What fees are included?
      iii)   Are there any annual fees?
      iv)   What is the post-introductory APR?

5)   Will you pay in full each month?

  a) No -- 0% APR card

      i)   How long does 0% APR term last?
      ii)   What fees are included?
      iii)   Are there any annual fees?
      iv)   What is the post-introductory APR?

  b) Yes – look for a cashback or reward card, go to question   6
for clarification

6)   Do you fly or stay in hotels a lot or plan to earn more
than 30,000 flight miles or 20 hotel nights each year?
Points are devalued annually.

      a)   No - go to question 7
      b)   Yes –airline or hotel rewards travel card

        i) Are there any annual fees?
        ii) What is APR?

7)   Do you want cash back or rewards?

      a)   Cash back – look for best cash back card – go to
question 8

      b)   Rewards - look for the reward you want – go to
question 8

8)   Do you plan to keep your card for more than 1 year?

      a)   No - focus on initial rewards or bonuses
      b)   Yes - look for the best ongoing rewards and
lowest fees, go to question 9

9)   Are you really organized? There are cards that offer
great rolling rewards. For instance, one month might be grocery stores
and the next be gas stations. You earn more with the monthly reward
category.

      a)   No – avoid card with rolling rewards
      b)   Yes – look for rolling rewards

As you compare credit card offers, look for the brand (Discover, Mastercard, Visa or American Express) based on your travel wishes.

Write down and compare APRs, introductory periods, annual fees, rewards, etc. Take your time to find the right one and then apply.

Credit Utilization Ratio

Credit utilization ratio looks at how much debt you have compared to how much revolving credit you have.

Add up all your credit limits on all your credit cards and any other revolving loans. Write that number here:___________

Add up all your debt on those credit cards. Write it here:________

Fill in the blanks: <u>debt</u> _________
                        credit_________

Divide debt by credit numbers, Hopefully, the number is less than 1. Write that number here:___________

Multiply that by 100 for a percentage. Write that number here:_________

Your goal is a credit utilization ratio of 30% or less.

And the example.

Debt $<u>1500</u> = 0.5
Income $2000

0.5 * 100 = 50%.

Records Storage

You'll need three file boxes or a three-drawer filing cabinet and a bunch of file folders. Box/drawer 1 is for Current Paperwork. Box/drawer 2 is for Shred By Date, and box/drawer 3 is for your Tax Related data.

Set up Box/Drawer 1

Current Box/drawer will contain this year's documents in the following folders:

- Credit card statement and receipts
- Car insurance policy and payment receipts
- Renter insurance policy and payment receipts
- Bank Statements and Slips
- Pay Stubs
- Cash receipts
- Investment statements
- Current loan information (one folder for each loan)
- Medical Bills
- Utility Bills
- Retirement plan statements
- Receipts for large ticket items attached to owner's manual and warranty info

Start by sorting all this year's paperwork into those categories. Sort older paperwork into the same categories but keep them separate.

Now Set Up Box/Drawer 2

Box/drawer 2 will contain all paperwork that needs to be shredded. If you are not certain what you should shred, shred anything with your name, address, financial information, personal information, etc. on it. Even envelopes! If you have any paperwork older than the shred by date, place them in the Shred this year file. Flies should include:

- Shred This Year

    ○ Canceled Insurance Policies – you should only have one of these files. Mark it as Insurance Policy shred this year.

- Files by Category and Year. You may have a number of these files. Keep statements separated by year and shred them on schedule.

    ○ Credit card statements (year), shred (three years later) For instance 2020, shred 2023

    ○ Investment statements (this year), shred (three years later)

    ○ Bank Statements (this year), shred (three years later)

    ○ Quarterly or monthly Investment statements (this year), shred (three years later)

    ○ Un-deducted Medical Bills (this year), shred (three years later)

    ○ Utility Bills (this year), shred (three years later)

    ○ Retirement plan statements (this year), shred (three years later)

    ○ Paid Off Loans (this year), shred (seven years later)

- Taxes

    ○ W2s – shred once you start getting Social Security

    ○ Retirement contributions, shred after retirement

    ○ Tax paperwork, by year, shred (seven years later)

Sort previous years' statements into the proper file.

Now Set Up Box/Drawer 3.

In box/drawer 3, you will keep anything related to paying taxes and all the tax paperwork and any communications you get from the IRS. You will have several files, so it may be easier to use a combination of file folders and manila envelopes.

- This Year's Taxes
  - Any communication from the IRS
  - Any of the following forms
  - IRS Notice 1444
  - Any form W-2, 1099, 1095, 1098, 5498
  - Any other tax forms mailed to you
- Tax deductible receipts or statements
- In-kind and cash donations
- Itemized qualified educational expenses
- Record of estimated tax payments made.
- Expenses related to your investments.
- State tax refund
- Records of any scholarships or fellowships you received.
- Amount of state and local income or sales tax paid (other than wage withholding)
- Invoice showing amount of vehicle sales tax paid and / or personal property tax on vehicles
- Other

If in doubt as to whether you need something for taxes, err on the side of caution and keep it.

After you file your taxes, remove the W2s and retirement contributions from the tax paperwork and place them in the correct files in the Shred Box.

Go Back to Box/Drawer 1

Go through each file and complete the following tasks:

- Credit card statement and receipts

  ○ Match receipts to statement and then place in the proper folder in Box/drawer 2.

  ○ Put any credit card statement with a tax related expense in the Other folder in box/drawer 3.

- Separate out old car and renter's policies from the current one if necessary and place in shred file.

- Bank Statements and Slips - match slips to statements and place slips in the proper shred folder

- Pay Stubs - match to your W-2 at the end of the year and place in the proper shred folder

- Cash receipts - once these are recorded in your budget, place in shred this year folder.

- Investment statements

  ○ Any purchases or sales go into the tax paperwork box for the current tax year.

- Current loan information (one folder for each loan)

- Medical Bills- if you are planning to deduct these, move them into the Tax box

- Utility Bills

- Retirement plan statements

- Receipts for large ticket items attached to owner's manual and warranty info

Woo hoo! Your paperwork is now organized, and it is fairly simple to keep up. The nice thing about this system is that you can just grab the appropriate file and shred it without having to sort through stacks of paperwork.

Advanced Directive Questions

If you plan to put an advanced directive or living will in place, your lawyer will ask questions that it helps to have thought about ahead of time. Your health care provider can help you to understand some of the finer points as well.

Young people generally do not die at statistically high rates. However, there are factors that you cannot account for – car accidents, cancer, violence, and even just plain bad luck. A living will helps your family to support your wishes.

This is not set in stone. You can change your mind and change your living will.

Your decisions are your own and should be respected. However, if you do not put them in writing, you will have to depend on someone to make decisions for you.

Who will be my proxy? This person speaks for you. This person needs to understand your wishes and be willing to fight for them if need be.

Blood transfusions are often a religious conviction. If you do not want blood transfusions or plasma or saline, make your wishes known.

Life support treatments can prolong life without necessarily giving any quality of life.
- You can state that you want ALL life support systems regardless of your situation.
- You can state you want NO life support regardless of whether or not it will prolong your life.
- You can choose the treatments you want, for instance:

a. Ventilator – these breathe for you but can have some serious complications

b. Tube feeding - this is a way for you to get nutrition if you are unable to eat

c. Dialysis –pulls waste material from your blood if your kidneys

Glossary

After-tax - you have already paid income tax on the money
APR or Annual Percentage Rate - how much interest you are charged a year by a lender

Assets -things you own that have resale value.

Bank - a company that handles financial services

Beneficiary - the person/people you name to receive your insurance or properties after your death

Budget -determines how much you should spend

Collateral -what you offer in exchange for a loan.

Collision -repairs or replaces your car if it is damaged by you in an accident

Comprehensive -covers your car for weather, theft, and other perils that do not happen when you are driving it

Contribution -money that you put in your retirement account

Co-pay - a fixed out-of-pocket amount you paid a health care provider for covered services.

Cosigning - you are accepting responsibility to pay back a loan

Credit limits - the maximum amount you can use on revolving loans

Credit report -documentation on how well you pay back loans

Credit scores -based on your credit report and estimate how well you pay back your loans

Credit union - a not-for-profit company that handles financial services

Credit utilization ratio - how much of your revolving credit you are using compared to how much you have

Debt to income ratios -compares your debts to your gross income

Deductible - a specified amount of money you pay before an insurance company will pay a claim

Deduction - money can be subtracted from your income tax

Defaulting - you do not make payments on a loan.

Dependent -someone who is dependent on you for shelter, food, etc. Usually children, but not always

Depreciation - the decrease in value of an asset over time.

Direct deposit - your employer electronically deposits your paycheck into your checking account

Discretionary spending -money spent on wants, not needs

Distribution - a monthly withdrawal from a retirement account

Equity - the difference between how much you owe on your house versus how much has been paid.

Exemptions - legal reductions that reduce the amount of taxable income. People often think exemptions = deductions, but they are not.

Expenditures - things you spend money on

FDIC - an insurance that repays money lost through a bank or credit union's loss of funds

FICA - Federal Insurance Contribution Act and represent federal payroll taxes

Grace period - the amount of time between when you buy using a credit card and when you must pay for it without getting interest charges

Gross pay - the entire amount you make before anything is taken out for taxes etc.

Hard pull - your entire credit report is released, with your permission.

HR or Human Resources - the people who maintain the paperwork that gets you hired, paid, and separated from the company

Inheritance - money, investments, or items you get from someone who has died.

Inheritance taxes - paid on property and money you receive from a will.

In-kind - non-cash gifts.

Interest - charge to use someone else's money.

IRA - Individual Retirement Account

IRS - the Internal Revenue Service, the federal government branch that collects taxes

Lemon - a piece of machinery that has defects that affect safety, value or utility

Liability - protects other people from your actions. You carry it to limit the odds of being sued.

Lien - an interest in something that grants partial ownership until the bill is paid. For instance, if you get a car fixed, the mechanic can have a lien on your car until the bill is paid in full. If you sell the car before paying your lien, you must pay the mechanic out of the proceeds.

Naturalized citizen - someone born outside the USA who is now a legal citizen of the US with voting privileges

Net pay - left over after taxes are taken out.

Not-for-profit companies - charities, public libraries, churches, etc. It is a legal definition

Overdraft - when you spend more money than is in your checking account and the bank covers the difference

Premium - paid by you to purchase an insurance policy

Pre-tax - the government has not collected taxes on your money.

Prime rate - the base interest rate that can be charged. It is set by the Fed or the Federal Reserve.

Principal - the actual amount of money you have borrowed.

Products - contracts between a financial business and a person

PTO - paid time off, can be used for vacation or sick time

Recall - issued by the manufacturer if there is a common defect with the product. The manufacturer will repair or replace the defective part

Revenue - money and other assets owned by a business or government

Revolving debt - debt you can use, pay off and reuse over and over

Rollover - moving 401K money into an IRA without being taxed

Routing number - your bank's electronic address. It is the first 9 numbers on your checks

Secured debt - debt that is secured with an asset or collateral

Social security - a federal program designed to provide retirement income and healthcare

Soft pulls - a limited amount of credit report information is released.

Tangible - you can touch it - a tangible good is a physical item. Labor is not considered tangible.

Tax preparer - a person trained to prepare, calculate and finalize income tax for someone else.

Taxes - charges imposed by a government to fund government spending

Unemployment or workers comp - pays part of income for people who are fired or laid off.

Unsecured debt - no collateral or asset backing it

Vested - that you have stayed at the company long enough to earn the retirement money in your company retirement account.

Worker's visa - gives non-citizens permission to legally work in the US

YTD - Year to Date

References

Bieber, Christy Rakoczy. "Getting a Loan with Bad Credit." *Creditkarma.com*, Credit Karma, 29 Mar. 2019, www.creditkarma.com/ personal-loans/i/loans-for-people-bad-credit.

Bloom, Ester. "No One Can Agree What 'Middle Class' Means, and It Might Matter Now More than Ever." *CNBC.com*, CNBC, 29 Oct. 2017, www.cnbc.com/2017/10/27/what-average-or-middle-class-american-means-matters-more-than-ever.html.

Broadley, Claire. "7 Ways to Spot a Fake Website before You Get Phished." *WhoIsHostingThis.com*, WhoIsHostingThis, 6 Aug. 2020, www.whoishostingthis.com/resources/spot-fake-website/.

Cassie. "9 of the Best Budget Planners You'll Obsess over in 2021." *Livinglowkey.com*, Living Low Key, 30 Nov. 2020, livinglowkey.com/best-budget-planner/.

"Checklist: Creating an Advance Health Care Directive." *Everplans.com*, Everplans, www.everplans.com/articles/checklist-creating-an-advance-health-care-directive.

"Common Money Mistakes | Fidelity." *Www.fidelity.com*, Fidelity, 6 Feb. 2020, www.fidelity.com/viewpoints/personal-finance/millennial-money-mistakes.

Corthern, Lance. "What Is the 50/30/20 Rule Budget & How Do I Use It?" *Creditkarma.com*, Credit Karma, 3 Jan. 2019, www.creditkarma.com/advice/i/50-30-20-rule/.

Epstein, Lita. "Credit Unions vs. Banks: 9 Ways to Decide Which Is Best for You." *Investopedia*, Investopedia, 2019, www.investopedia.com/ credit-unions-vs-banks-4590218.

Fontinelle, Amy. "10 Reasons to Use Your Credit Card." *Investopedia.com*, Investopedia, 10 Oct. 2019, www.investopedia.com/articles/pf/10/ credit-card-debit-card.asp.

"Free Budget Planner Worksheets." *Nationaldebtrelief.com*, National Debt Relief, www.nationaldebtrelief.com/free-budget-planner-worksheet

Hagen, Kailey. "The Real Cost of Only Making Your Credit Card's Minimum Payment." *Fool.com*, The Motley Fool, 31 Mar. 2020, www.fool.com/ the-ascent/credit-cards/articles/real-cost-of-only-making-your-credit-cards-minimum-payment/.

---. "Which Type of Retirement Plan Is Right for You?" *Fool.com*, The Motley Fool, 6 Jan. 2021, www.fool.com/retirement/2017/05/09/how-long-will-my-retirement-savings-last.aspx.

Hayes, Adam. "Debt Ratio." *Investopedia.com*, Investopedia, 1 June 2020, www.investopedia.com/terms/d/debtratio.asp.

Horvath, Sarah. "The Best Free or Low-Cost Budget Spreadsheets for 2021." *Benzinga.com*, Benzinga, 14 Oct. 2020, www.benzinga.com/money/best-budget-spreadsheets/.

"How to Avoid Holiday Scams." *Takechargeamerica.org*, Take Charge America, 16 May 2014, www.takechargeamerica.org/

Huddleston, Cameron. "Pros and Cons of Life Insurance for Children." *Forbes.com,* Forbes, 19 Oct. 2020, www.forbes.com/advisor/life-insurance/life-insurance-for-children/.

Irby, Latoya. "Paying off Debt: Minimum Payment, Maximum Cost." *Thebalance.com/*, The Balance, 31 Jan. 2020, www.thebalance.com/how-long-to-pay-off-balance-with-minimum-payments-961120.

Jayakumar, Amrita. "Credit Lock vs. Credit Freeze: What's the Difference?" *NerdWallet.com*, NerdWallet, 3 Dec. 2020, www.nerdwallet.com/article/finance/credit-lock-and-credit-freeze.

Johansen, Allison Grace. "Norton." *Norton.com*, Norton Life Lock, 2019, us.norton.com/internetsecurity-emerging-threats-what-to-do-after-a-data-breach.html.

Kennon, Joshua. "Investment Terms Everyone Should Know." *The Balance*, The Balance, 19 May 2020, www.thebalance.com/investing-terms-you-should-know-356338.

Kiernan, John S. "What Credit Card Should I Get? Top Picks by Category." *WalletHub.com*, WalletHub, 3 Jan. 2020, wallethub.com/edu/cc/what-credit-card-should-i-get/41761/.

---. "What Credit Score Do You Start With?" *WalletHub.com*, Wallet Hub, 15 Feb. 2016, wallethub.com/edu/cs/what-does-your-credit-score-start-at/19258.

Kinney, Jeff. "Best Renters Insurance Companies of 2021." *Usnews.com*, US News and World Report, 14 May 2020, www.usnews.com/360-reviews/renters-insurance/best-renters-insurance-companies.

Kurt, Daniel. "Should I Get a Credit Card?" *Investopedia.com*, Investopedia, 7 Dec. 2020, www.investopedia.com/should-i-get-a-credit-card-4589811.

Leonhardt, Megan. "5 Steps to Take If You Suspect You Were Affected by the MGM Resort Data Breach." *CNBC.com*, CNBC, 20 Feb. 2020, www.cnbc.com/2020/02/20/mgm-data-breach-5-things-you-should-do-if-you-were-affected.html.

Longley, Robert. "What Is Profit Sharing? Pros and Cons." *ThoughtCo.com*, ThoughtCo, 14 Aug. 2019, www.thoughtco.com/what-is-profit-sharing-4692535.

Luthi, Ben. "How to Pick the Right Credit Card for You." *Www.experian.com*, Experian, 16 Jan. 2020, www.experian.com/blogs/ask-experian/what-credit-card-should-i-get/.

Majidi, Fran. "Do You Live in a No Fault State or a Tort Law Insurance State?" *SmartFinancial.com*, Smart Financial, 2 May 2019, smartfinancial.com/No-Fault-State-or-Tort-Law-Insurance-State.

Marquit, Miranda. "Investment Terms and Definitions You Should Know." *Investorjunkie.com*, Investorjunkie, 2 Dec. 2020, investorjunkie.com/investing/common-investing-terms-definitions/.

O'Shea, Arielle. "The 7 Best Budget Apps and Personal Finance Tools for 2019." *NerdWallet,Com*, NerdWallet, 13 Mar. 2019, www.nerdwallet.com/blog/finance/budgeting-saving-tools/.

Pomroy, Kathryn. "Average Stock Market Return: Where Does 7% Come From?" *TheSimpleDollar.com*, The Simple Dollar, 14 Apr. 2013, www.thesimpledollar.com/investing/stocks/where-does-7-come-from-when-it-comes-to-long-term-stock-returns/.

Probasco, Jim. "How Much Do I Need to Retire?" *Investopedia.com*, Investopedia, 22 Dec. 2020, www.investopedia.com/retirement/how-much-you-should-have-saved-age/.

Schroeder-Gardner, Michelle. "11 Questions to Ask Yourself before a Large Purchase." *Makingsenseofcents.com*, Making Sense Of Cents, 31 Aug. 2016, www.makingsenseofcents.com/2016/08/what-to-do-before-a-large-purchase.html.

Sellery, Bruce. "What Happens If Your Co-Signer Dies?" *MoneySense.ca*, Money Sense, 26 Sept. 2012, www.moneysense.ca/columns/what-happens-if-your-co-signer-dies/#:~:text=Co-signing

Sember, Brette. "The Probate Process: Four Simple Steps." *Legalzoom.com*, LegalZoom, 23 Dec. 2020, www.legalzoom.com/articles/the-probate-process-four-simple-steps#

Solutions, Ramsey. "Bank Fees: Everything Your Bank Can Charge You For." *Daveramsey.com*, Dave Ramsey, 13 Aug. 2020, www.daveramsey.com/blog/bank-fees.

Urie, Daniel. "Don't Be a Victim: Tips for Avoiding Scams This Holiday
        Shopping Season." *Pennlive.com*, PennLive, 26 Oct. 2020,
        www.pennlive.com/life/2020/10/avoid-scammers-this-holiday-
        shopping-season-with-these-tips.html.
Vansomeren, Lindsay. "How to Manage Your Budget Using the 50/30/20
        Budgeting Rule." *Thebalance.com*, The Balance, 15 Jan. 2021,
        www.thebalance.com/the-50-30-20-rule-of-thumb-453922.
"What Is a Debt-To-Income Ratio? Why Is the 43% Debt-To-Income Ratio
        Important?" *Consumerfinance.gov*, Consumer Financial Protection
        Bureau, 15 Nov. 2019, www.consumerfinance.gov/ask-cfpb/what-is-
        a-debt-to-income-ratio-why-is-the-43-debt-to-income-ratio-
        important-en-1791/.
"What Should Your Retirement Savings Look like Right
        Now?" *Nationaldebtrelief.com*, National Debt Relief, 27 Aug. 2020,
        www.nationaldebtrelief.com/retirement-savings/.
White, Alexandria. "25 Key Terms Everyone with a Credit Card Should
        Know." *CNBC.com*, CNBC, 15 Oct. 2019, www.cnbc.com/select/
        common-credit-card-terms/.

About the Author and Illustrator

Marjorie Daley lives in Wyoming with her husband Bob, horse Penny, naughty dog Diesel and permanent foster dog, Tira, and assorted small pets. Her writing passion is Wyoming history, but she is happy to tackle almost any subject.

- Facebook: Marjorie-Daley-author
- http://marjorie-reflections.blogspot.com/

Madora Daley-Green is a studio art major at the University of Wyoming. They plan to work in manga and graphic novels. Check out their work at @ladyspottedray on Twitter, Instagram, and Tumblr

Also by Marjorie Daley

An Unorthodox War

Fire Ground

Naughty Dogs: Identifying, Diagnosing, Understanding, and Correcting Your Dog's Unwanted Behaviors

The Ultimate Guide to Wild Canines, Primitive Dogs, and Pariah Dogs: An Owner's Guidebook for Wolfdogs, Coydogs, and Other Hereditarily Wild Dog Breeds

Printed in the United States